# THIS BOOK BELONGS TO:

| CONTACT INFORMATION | |
|---|---|
| NAME: | |
| ADDRESS: | |
| PHONE: | |

START / END DATES

___ / ___ / ___   TO   ___ / ___ / ___

## HOW TO USE THIS BOOK:

The purpose of this book is to keep all of your movie watching experiences and findings all in one place. It will help keep you organized.

This Movie Log Book will allow you to accurately document all the things you want to remember about your experience of watching films and movies. It's a great way to chart your course through the world of movies.

Here are examples of the prompts for you to fill in and write about your experience and findings in this book:

1. Movie Title - Name of the movie.
2. Genre - Record which particular genre or specific category the movie falls under.
3. Date Watched - Write the date you watch the movie.
4. Rating - Rate the movie from 1-5 stars.
5. Notes - Write any important details you want to remember such as actors, director, scene information, personal or professional use, was the movie creative, quotes or highlights from the movie, how was the script, etc.

# My Movie Tracker

| MOVIE TITLE | | DATE WATCHED | |
|---|---|---|---|
| GENRE | | RATING | ☆ ☆ ☆ ☆ ☆ |
| NOTES | | | |

| MOVIE TITLE | | DATE WATCHED | |
|---|---|---|---|
| GENRE | | RATING | ☆ ☆ ☆ ☆ ☆ |
| NOTES | | | |

| MOVIE TITLE | | DATE WATCHED | |
|---|---|---|---|
| GENRE | | RATING | ☆ ☆ ☆ ☆ ☆ |
| NOTES | | | |

| MOVIE TITLE | | DATE WATCHED | |
|---|---|---|---|
| GENRE | | RATING | ☆ ☆ ☆ ☆ ☆ |
| NOTES | | | |

| MOVIE TITLE | | DATE WATCHED | |
|---|---|---|---|
| GENRE | | RATING | ☆ ☆ ☆ ☆ ☆ |
| NOTES | | | |

| MOVIE TITLE | | DATE WATCHED | |
|---|---|---|---|
| GENRE | | RATING | ☆ ☆ ☆ ☆ ☆ |
| NOTES | | | |

| MOVIE TITLE | | DATE WATCHED | |
|---|---|---|---|
| GENRE | | RATING | ☆ ☆ ☆ ☆ ☆ |
| NOTES | | | |

| MOVIE TITLE | | DATE WATCHED | |
|---|---|---|---|
| GENRE | | RATING | ☆ ☆ ☆ ☆ ☆ |
| NOTES | | | |

# My Movie Tracker

| MOVIE TITLE | | DATE WATCHED | |
|---|---|---|---|
| GENRE | | RATING | ☆ ☆ ☆ ☆ ☆ |
| NOTES | | | |

| MOVIE TITLE | | DATE WATCHED | |
|---|---|---|---|
| GENRE | | RATING | ☆ ☆ ☆ ☆ ☆ |
| NOTES | | | |

| MOVIE TITLE | | DATE WATCHED | |
|---|---|---|---|
| GENRE | | RATING | ☆ ☆ ☆ ☆ ☆ |
| NOTES | | | |

| MOVIE TITLE | | DATE WATCHED | |
|---|---|---|---|
| GENRE | | RATING | ☆ ☆ ☆ ☆ ☆ |
| NOTES | | | |

| MOVIE TITLE | | DATE WATCHED | |
|---|---|---|---|
| GENRE | | RATING | ☆ ☆ ☆ ☆ ☆ |
| NOTES | | | |

| MOVIE TITLE | | DATE WATCHED | |
|---|---|---|---|
| GENRE | | RATING | ☆ ☆ ☆ ☆ ☆ |
| NOTES | | | |

| MOVIE TITLE | | DATE WATCHED | |
|---|---|---|---|
| GENRE | | RATING | ☆ ☆ ☆ ☆ ☆ |
| NOTES | | | |

| MOVIE TITLE | | DATE WATCHED | |
|---|---|---|---|
| GENRE | | RATING | ☆ ☆ ☆ ☆ ☆ |
| NOTES | | | |

# My Movie Tracker

| MOVIE TITLE | | DATE WATCHED | |
|---|---|---|---|
| GENRE | | RATING | ☆ ☆ ☆ ☆ ☆ |
| NOTES | | | |

| MOVIE TITLE | | DATE WATCHED | |
|---|---|---|---|
| GENRE | | RATING | ☆ ☆ ☆ ☆ ☆ |
| NOTES | | | |

| MOVIE TITLE | | DATE WATCHED | |
|---|---|---|---|
| GENRE | | RATING | ☆ ☆ ☆ ☆ ☆ |
| NOTES | | | |

| MOVIE TITLE | | DATE WATCHED | |
|---|---|---|---|
| GENRE | | RATING | ☆ ☆ ☆ ☆ ☆ |
| NOTES | | | |

| MOVIE TITLE | | DATE WATCHED | |
|---|---|---|---|
| GENRE | | RATING | ☆ ☆ ☆ ☆ ☆ |
| NOTES | | | |

| MOVIE TITLE | | DATE WATCHED | |
|---|---|---|---|
| GENRE | | RATING | ☆ ☆ ☆ ☆ ☆ |
| NOTES | | | |

| MOVIE TITLE | | DATE WATCHED | |
|---|---|---|---|
| GENRE | | RATING | ☆ ☆ ☆ ☆ ☆ |
| NOTES | | | |

| MOVIE TITLE | | DATE WATCHED | |
|---|---|---|---|
| GENRE | | RATING | ☆ ☆ ☆ ☆ ☆ |
| NOTES | | | |

# My Movie Tracker

| MOVIE TITLE | | DATE WATCHED | |
|---|---|---|---|
| GENRE | | RATING | ☆ ☆ ☆ ☆ ☆ |
| NOTES | | | |

| MOVIE TITLE | | DATE WATCHED | |
|---|---|---|---|
| GENRE | | RATING | ☆ ☆ ☆ ☆ ☆ |
| NOTES | | | |

| MOVIE TITLE | | DATE WATCHED | |
|---|---|---|---|
| GENRE | | RATING | ☆ ☆ ☆ ☆ ☆ |
| NOTES | | | |

| MOVIE TITLE | | DATE WATCHED | |
|---|---|---|---|
| GENRE | | RATING | ☆ ☆ ☆ ☆ ☆ |
| NOTES | | | |

| MOVIE TITLE | | DATE WATCHED | |
|---|---|---|---|
| GENRE | | RATING | ☆ ☆ ☆ ☆ ☆ |
| NOTES | | | |

| MOVIE TITLE | | DATE WATCHED | |
|---|---|---|---|
| GENRE | | RATING | ☆ ☆ ☆ ☆ ☆ |
| NOTES | | | |

| MOVIE TITLE | | DATE WATCHED | |
|---|---|---|---|
| GENRE | | RATING | ☆ ☆ ☆ ☆ ☆ |
| NOTES | | | |

| MOVIE TITLE | | DATE WATCHED | |
|---|---|---|---|
| GENRE | | RATING | ☆ ☆ ☆ ☆ ☆ |
| NOTES | | | |

# My Movie Tracker

| MOVIE TITLE | | DATE WATCHED | |
|---|---|---|---|
| GENRE | | RATING | ☆ ☆ ☆ ☆ ☆ |
| NOTES | | | |

| MOVIE TITLE | | DATE WATCHED | |
|---|---|---|---|
| GENRE | | RATING | ☆ ☆ ☆ ☆ ☆ |
| NOTES | | | |

| MOVIE TITLE | | DATE WATCHED | |
|---|---|---|---|
| GENRE | | RATING | ☆ ☆ ☆ ☆ ☆ |
| NOTES | | | |

| MOVIE TITLE | | DATE WATCHED | |
|---|---|---|---|
| GENRE | | RATING | ☆ ☆ ☆ ☆ ☆ |
| NOTES | | | |

| MOVIE TITLE | | DATE WATCHED | |
|---|---|---|---|
| GENRE | | RATING | ☆ ☆ ☆ ☆ ☆ |
| NOTES | | | |

| MOVIE TITLE | | DATE WATCHED | |
|---|---|---|---|
| GENRE | | RATING | ☆ ☆ ☆ ☆ ☆ |
| NOTES | | | |

| MOVIE TITLE | | DATE WATCHED | |
|---|---|---|---|
| GENRE | | RATING | ☆ ☆ ☆ ☆ ☆ |
| NOTES | | | |

| MOVIE TITLE | | DATE WATCHED | |
|---|---|---|---|
| GENRE | | RATING | ☆ ☆ ☆ ☆ ☆ |
| NOTES | | | |

# My Movie Tracker

| MOVIE TITLE | | DATE WATCHED | |
|---|---|---|---|
| GENRE | | RATING | ☆ ☆ ☆ ☆ ☆ |
| NOTES | | | |

| MOVIE TITLE | | DATE WATCHED | |
|---|---|---|---|
| GENRE | | RATING | ☆ ☆ ☆ ☆ ☆ |
| NOTES | | | |

| MOVIE TITLE | | DATE WATCHED | |
|---|---|---|---|
| GENRE | | RATING | ☆ ☆ ☆ ☆ ☆ |
| NOTES | | | |

| MOVIE TITLE | | DATE WATCHED | |
|---|---|---|---|
| GENRE | | RATING | ☆ ☆ ☆ ☆ ☆ |
| NOTES | | | |

| MOVIE TITLE | | DATE WATCHED | |
|---|---|---|---|
| GENRE | | RATING | ☆ ☆ ☆ ☆ ☆ |
| NOTES | | | |

| MOVIE TITLE | | DATE WATCHED | |
|---|---|---|---|
| GENRE | | RATING | ☆ ☆ ☆ ☆ ☆ |
| NOTES | | | |

| MOVIE TITLE | | DATE WATCHED | |
|---|---|---|---|
| GENRE | | RATING | ☆ ☆ ☆ ☆ ☆ |
| NOTES | | | |

| MOVIE TITLE | | DATE WATCHED | |
|---|---|---|---|
| GENRE | | RATING | ☆ ☆ ☆ ☆ ☆ |
| NOTES | | | |

# My Movie Tracker

| MOVIE TITLE | | DATE WATCHED | |
|---|---|---|---|
| GENRE | | RATING | ☆ ☆ ☆ ☆ ☆ |
| NOTES | | | |

| MOVIE TITLE | | DATE WATCHED | |
|---|---|---|---|
| GENRE | | RATING | ☆ ☆ ☆ ☆ ☆ |
| NOTES | | | |

| MOVIE TITLE | | DATE WATCHED | |
|---|---|---|---|
| GENRE | | RATING | ☆ ☆ ☆ ☆ ☆ |
| NOTES | | | |

| MOVIE TITLE | | DATE WATCHED | |
|---|---|---|---|
| GENRE | | RATING | ☆ ☆ ☆ ☆ ☆ |
| NOTES | | | |

| MOVIE TITLE | | DATE WATCHED | |
|---|---|---|---|
| GENRE | | RATING | ☆ ☆ ☆ ☆ ☆ |
| NOTES | | | |

| MOVIE TITLE | | DATE WATCHED | |
|---|---|---|---|
| GENRE | | RATING | ☆ ☆ ☆ ☆ ☆ |
| NOTES | | | |

| MOVIE TITLE | | DATE WATCHED | |
|---|---|---|---|
| GENRE | | RATING | ☆ ☆ ☆ ☆ ☆ |
| NOTES | | | |

| MOVIE TITLE | | DATE WATCHED | |
|---|---|---|---|
| GENRE | | RATING | ☆ ☆ ☆ ☆ ☆ |
| NOTES | | | |

# My Movie Tracker

| MOVIE TITLE | | DATE WATCHED | |
|---|---|---|---|
| GENRE | | RATING | ☆ ☆ ☆ ☆ ☆ |
| NOTES | | | |

| MOVIE TITLE | | DATE WATCHED | |
|---|---|---|---|
| GENRE | | RATING | ☆ ☆ ☆ ☆ ☆ |
| NOTES | | | |

| MOVIE TITLE | | DATE WATCHED | |
|---|---|---|---|
| GENRE | | RATING | ☆ ☆ ☆ ☆ ☆ |
| NOTES | | | |

| MOVIE TITLE | | DATE WATCHED | |
|---|---|---|---|
| GENRE | | RATING | ☆ ☆ ☆ ☆ ☆ |
| NOTES | | | |

| MOVIE TITLE | | DATE WATCHED | |
|---|---|---|---|
| GENRE | | RATING | ☆ ☆ ☆ ☆ ☆ |
| NOTES | | | |

| MOVIE TITLE | | DATE WATCHED | |
|---|---|---|---|
| GENRE | | RATING | ☆ ☆ ☆ ☆ ☆ |
| NOTES | | | |

| MOVIE TITLE | | DATE WATCHED | |
|---|---|---|---|
| GENRE | | RATING | ☆ ☆ ☆ ☆ ☆ |
| NOTES | | | |

| MOVIE TITLE | | DATE WATCHED | |
|---|---|---|---|
| GENRE | | RATING | ☆ ☆ ☆ ☆ ☆ |
| NOTES | | | |

# My Movie Tracker

| MOVIE TITLE | | DATE WATCHED | |
|---|---|---|---|
| GENRE | | RATING | ☆ ☆ ☆ ☆ ☆ |
| NOTES | | | |

| MOVIE TITLE | | DATE WATCHED | |
|---|---|---|---|
| GENRE | | RATING | ☆ ☆ ☆ ☆ ☆ |
| NOTES | | | |

| MOVIE TITLE | | DATE WATCHED | |
|---|---|---|---|
| GENRE | | RATING | ☆ ☆ ☆ ☆ ☆ |
| NOTES | | | |

| MOVIE TITLE | | DATE WATCHED | |
|---|---|---|---|
| GENRE | | RATING | ☆ ☆ ☆ ☆ ☆ |
| NOTES | | | |

| MOVIE TITLE | | DATE WATCHED | |
|---|---|---|---|
| GENRE | | RATING | ☆ ☆ ☆ ☆ ☆ |
| NOTES | | | |

| MOVIE TITLE | | DATE WATCHED | |
|---|---|---|---|
| GENRE | | RATING | ☆ ☆ ☆ ☆ ☆ |
| NOTES | | | |

| MOVIE TITLE | | DATE WATCHED | |
|---|---|---|---|
| GENRE | | RATING | ☆ ☆ ☆ ☆ ☆ |
| NOTES | | | |

| MOVIE TITLE | | DATE WATCHED | |
|---|---|---|---|
| GENRE | | RATING | ☆ ☆ ☆ ☆ ☆ |
| NOTES | | | |

# My Movie Tracker

| MOVIE TITLE | | DATE WATCHED | |
|---|---|---|---|
| GENRE | | RATING | ☆ ☆ ☆ ☆ ☆ |
| NOTES | | | |

| MOVIE TITLE | | DATE WATCHED | |
|---|---|---|---|
| GENRE | | RATING | ☆ ☆ ☆ ☆ ☆ |
| NOTES | | | |

| MOVIE TITLE | | DATE WATCHED | |
|---|---|---|---|
| GENRE | | RATING | ☆ ☆ ☆ ☆ ☆ |
| NOTES | | | |

| MOVIE TITLE | | DATE WATCHED | |
|---|---|---|---|
| GENRE | | RATING | ☆ ☆ ☆ ☆ ☆ |
| NOTES | | | |

| MOVIE TITLE | | DATE WATCHED | |
|---|---|---|---|
| GENRE | | RATING | ☆ ☆ ☆ ☆ ☆ |
| NOTES | | | |

| MOVIE TITLE | | DATE WATCHED | |
|---|---|---|---|
| GENRE | | RATING | ☆ ☆ ☆ ☆ ☆ |
| NOTES | | | |

| MOVIE TITLE | | DATE WATCHED | |
|---|---|---|---|
| GENRE | | RATING | ☆ ☆ ☆ ☆ ☆ |
| NOTES | | | |

| MOVIE TITLE | | DATE WATCHED | |
|---|---|---|---|
| GENRE | | RATING | ☆ ☆ ☆ ☆ ☆ |
| NOTES | | | |

# My Movie Tracker

| MOVIE TITLE | | DATE WATCHED | |
|---|---|---|---|
| GENRE | | RATING | ☆ ☆ ☆ ☆ ☆ |
| NOTES | | | |

| MOVIE TITLE | | DATE WATCHED | |
|---|---|---|---|
| GENRE | | RATING | ☆ ☆ ☆ ☆ ☆ |
| NOTES | | | |

| MOVIE TITLE | | DATE WATCHED | |
|---|---|---|---|
| GENRE | | RATING | ☆ ☆ ☆ ☆ ☆ |
| NOTES | | | |

| MOVIE TITLE | | DATE WATCHED | |
|---|---|---|---|
| GENRE | | RATING | ☆ ☆ ☆ ☆ ☆ |
| NOTES | | | |

| MOVIE TITLE | | DATE WATCHED | |
|---|---|---|---|
| GENRE | | RATING | ☆ ☆ ☆ ☆ ☆ |
| NOTES | | | |

| MOVIE TITLE | | DATE WATCHED | |
|---|---|---|---|
| GENRE | | RATING | ☆ ☆ ☆ ☆ ☆ |
| NOTES | | | |

| MOVIE TITLE | | DATE WATCHED | |
|---|---|---|---|
| GENRE | | RATING | ☆ ☆ ☆ ☆ ☆ |
| NOTES | | | |

| MOVIE TITLE | | DATE WATCHED | |
|---|---|---|---|
| GENRE | | RATING | ☆ ☆ ☆ ☆ ☆ |
| NOTES | | | |

# My Movie Tracker

| MOVIE TITLE | | DATE WATCHED | |
|---|---|---|---|
| GENRE | | RATING | ☆ ☆ ☆ ☆ ☆ |
| NOTES | | | |

| MOVIE TITLE | | DATE WATCHED | |
|---|---|---|---|
| GENRE | | RATING | ☆ ☆ ☆ ☆ ☆ |
| NOTES | | | |

| MOVIE TITLE | | DATE WATCHED | |
|---|---|---|---|
| GENRE | | RATING | ☆ ☆ ☆ ☆ ☆ |
| NOTES | | | |

| MOVIE TITLE | | DATE WATCHED | |
|---|---|---|---|
| GENRE | | RATING | ☆ ☆ ☆ ☆ ☆ |
| NOTES | | | |

| MOVIE TITLE | | DATE WATCHED | |
|---|---|---|---|
| GENRE | | RATING | ☆ ☆ ☆ ☆ ☆ |
| NOTES | | | |

| MOVIE TITLE | | DATE WATCHED | |
|---|---|---|---|
| GENRE | | RATING | ☆ ☆ ☆ ☆ ☆ |
| NOTES | | | |

| MOVIE TITLE | | DATE WATCHED | |
|---|---|---|---|
| GENRE | | RATING | ☆ ☆ ☆ ☆ ☆ |
| NOTES | | | |

| MOVIE TITLE | | DATE WATCHED | |
|---|---|---|---|
| GENRE | | RATING | ☆ ☆ ☆ ☆ ☆ |
| NOTES | | | |

# My Movie Tracker

| MOVIE TITLE | | DATE WATCHED | |
|---|---|---|---|
| GENRE | | RATING | ☆ ☆ ☆ ☆ ☆ |
| NOTES | | | |

| MOVIE TITLE | | DATE WATCHED | |
|---|---|---|---|
| GENRE | | RATING | ☆ ☆ ☆ ☆ ☆ |
| NOTES | | | |

| MOVIE TITLE | | DATE WATCHED | |
|---|---|---|---|
| GENRE | | RATING | ☆ ☆ ☆ ☆ ☆ |
| NOTES | | | |

| MOVIE TITLE | | DATE WATCHED | |
|---|---|---|---|
| GENRE | | RATING | ☆ ☆ ☆ ☆ ☆ |
| NOTES | | | |

| MOVIE TITLE | | DATE WATCHED | |
|---|---|---|---|
| GENRE | | RATING | ☆ ☆ ☆ ☆ ☆ |
| NOTES | | | |

| MOVIE TITLE | | DATE WATCHED | |
|---|---|---|---|
| GENRE | | RATING | ☆ ☆ ☆ ☆ ☆ |
| NOTES | | | |

| MOVIE TITLE | | DATE WATCHED | |
|---|---|---|---|
| GENRE | | RATING | ☆ ☆ ☆ ☆ ☆ |
| NOTES | | | |

| MOVIE TITLE | | DATE WATCHED | |
|---|---|---|---|
| GENRE | | RATING | ☆ ☆ ☆ ☆ ☆ |
| NOTES | | | |

# My Movie Tracker

| MOVIE TITLE | | DATE WATCHED | |
|---|---|---|---|
| GENRE | | RATING | ☆ ☆ ☆ ☆ ☆ |
| NOTES | | | |

| MOVIE TITLE | | DATE WATCHED | |
|---|---|---|---|
| GENRE | | RATING | ☆ ☆ ☆ ☆ ☆ |
| NOTES | | | |

| MOVIE TITLE | | DATE WATCHED | |
|---|---|---|---|
| GENRE | | RATING | ☆ ☆ ☆ ☆ ☆ |
| NOTES | | | |

| MOVIE TITLE | | DATE WATCHED | |
|---|---|---|---|
| GENRE | | RATING | ☆ ☆ ☆ ☆ ☆ |
| NOTES | | | |

| MOVIE TITLE | | DATE WATCHED | |
|---|---|---|---|
| GENRE | | RATING | ☆ ☆ ☆ ☆ ☆ |
| NOTES | | | |

| MOVIE TITLE | | DATE WATCHED | |
|---|---|---|---|
| GENRE | | RATING | ☆ ☆ ☆ ☆ ☆ |
| NOTES | | | |

| MOVIE TITLE | | DATE WATCHED | |
|---|---|---|---|
| GENRE | | RATING | ☆ ☆ ☆ ☆ ☆ |
| NOTES | | | |

| MOVIE TITLE | | DATE WATCHED | |
|---|---|---|---|
| GENRE | | RATING | ☆ ☆ ☆ ☆ ☆ |
| NOTES | | | |

# My Movie Tracker

| MOVIE TITLE | | DATE WATCHED | |
|---|---|---|---|
| GENRE | | RATING | ☆ ☆ ☆ ☆ ☆ |
| NOTES | | | |

| MOVIE TITLE | | DATE WATCHED | |
|---|---|---|---|
| GENRE | | RATING | ☆ ☆ ☆ ☆ ☆ |
| NOTES | | | |

| MOVIE TITLE | | DATE WATCHED | |
|---|---|---|---|
| GENRE | | RATING | ☆ ☆ ☆ ☆ ☆ |
| NOTES | | | |

| MOVIE TITLE | | DATE WATCHED | |
|---|---|---|---|
| GENRE | | RATING | ☆ ☆ ☆ ☆ ☆ |
| NOTES | | | |

| MOVIE TITLE | | DATE WATCHED | |
|---|---|---|---|
| GENRE | | RATING | ☆ ☆ ☆ ☆ ☆ |
| NOTES | | | |

| MOVIE TITLE | | DATE WATCHED | |
|---|---|---|---|
| GENRE | | RATING | ☆ ☆ ☆ ☆ ☆ |
| NOTES | | | |

| MOVIE TITLE | | DATE WATCHED | |
|---|---|---|---|
| GENRE | | RATING | ☆ ☆ ☆ ☆ ☆ |
| NOTES | | | |

| MOVIE TITLE | | DATE WATCHED | |
|---|---|---|---|
| GENRE | | RATING | ☆ ☆ ☆ ☆ ☆ |
| NOTES | | | |

# My Movie Tracker

| MOVIE TITLE | | DATE WATCHED | |
|---|---|---|---|
| GENRE | | RATING | ☆ ☆ ☆ ☆ ☆ |
| NOTES | | | |

| MOVIE TITLE | | DATE WATCHED | |
|---|---|---|---|
| GENRE | | RATING | ☆ ☆ ☆ ☆ ☆ |
| NOTES | | | |

| MOVIE TITLE | | DATE WATCHED | |
|---|---|---|---|
| GENRE | | RATING | ☆ ☆ ☆ ☆ ☆ |
| NOTES | | | |

| MOVIE TITLE | | DATE WATCHED | |
|---|---|---|---|
| GENRE | | RATING | ☆ ☆ ☆ ☆ ☆ |
| NOTES | | | |

| MOVIE TITLE | | DATE WATCHED | |
|---|---|---|---|
| GENRE | | RATING | ☆ ☆ ☆ ☆ ☆ |
| NOTES | | | |

| MOVIE TITLE | | DATE WATCHED | |
|---|---|---|---|
| GENRE | | RATING | ☆ ☆ ☆ ☆ ☆ |
| NOTES | | | |

| MOVIE TITLE | | DATE WATCHED | |
|---|---|---|---|
| GENRE | | RATING | ☆ ☆ ☆ ☆ ☆ |
| NOTES | | | |

| MOVIE TITLE | | DATE WATCHED | |
|---|---|---|---|
| GENRE | | RATING | ☆ ☆ ☆ ☆ ☆ |
| NOTES | | | |

# My Movie Tracker

| MOVIE TITLE | | DATE WATCHED | |
|---|---|---|---|
| GENRE | | RATING | ☆ ☆ ☆ ☆ ☆ |
| NOTES | | | |

| MOVIE TITLE | | DATE WATCHED | |
|---|---|---|---|
| GENRE | | RATING | ☆ ☆ ☆ ☆ ☆ |
| NOTES | | | |

| MOVIE TITLE | | DATE WATCHED | |
|---|---|---|---|
| GENRE | | RATING | ☆ ☆ ☆ ☆ ☆ |
| NOTES | | | |

| MOVIE TITLE | | DATE WATCHED | |
|---|---|---|---|
| GENRE | | RATING | ☆ ☆ ☆ ☆ ☆ |
| NOTES | | | |

| MOVIE TITLE | | DATE WATCHED | |
|---|---|---|---|
| GENRE | | RATING | ☆ ☆ ☆ ☆ ☆ |
| NOTES | | | |

| MOVIE TITLE | | DATE WATCHED | |
|---|---|---|---|
| GENRE | | RATING | ☆ ☆ ☆ ☆ ☆ |
| NOTES | | | |

| MOVIE TITLE | | DATE WATCHED | |
|---|---|---|---|
| GENRE | | RATING | ☆ ☆ ☆ ☆ ☆ |
| NOTES | | | |

| MOVIE TITLE | | DATE WATCHED | |
|---|---|---|---|
| GENRE | | RATING | ☆ ☆ ☆ ☆ |
| NOTES | | | |

# My Movie Tracker

| MOVIE TITLE | | DATE WATCHED | |
|---|---|---|---|
| GENRE | | RATING | ☆ ☆ ☆ ☆ ☆ |
| NOTES | | | |

| MOVIE TITLE | | DATE WATCHED | |
|---|---|---|---|
| GENRE | | RATING | ☆ ☆ ☆ ☆ ☆ |
| NOTES | | | |

| MOVIE TITLE | | DATE WATCHED | |
|---|---|---|---|
| GENRE | | RATING | ☆ ☆ ☆ ☆ ☆ |
| NOTES | | | |

| MOVIE TITLE | | DATE WATCHED | |
|---|---|---|---|
| GENRE | | RATING | ☆ ☆ ☆ ☆ ☆ |
| NOTES | | | |

| MOVIE TITLE | | DATE WATCHED | |
|---|---|---|---|
| GENRE | | RATING | ☆ ☆ ☆ ☆ ☆ |
| NOTES | | | |

| MOVIE TITLE | | DATE WATCHED | |
|---|---|---|---|
| GENRE | | RATING | ☆ ☆ ☆ ☆ ☆ |
| NOTES | | | |

| MOVIE TITLE | | DATE WATCHED | |
|---|---|---|---|
| GENRE | | RATING | ☆ ☆ ☆ ☆ ☆ |
| NOTES | | | |

| MOVIE TITLE | | DATE WATCHED | |
|---|---|---|---|
| GENRE | | RATING | ☆ ☆ ☆ ☆ ☆ |
| NOTES | | | |

# My Movie Tracker

| MOVIE TITLE | | DATE WATCHED | |
|---|---|---|---|
| GENRE | | RATING | ★ ★ ★ ★ ★ |
| NOTES | | | |

| MOVIE TITLE | | DATE WATCHED | |
|---|---|---|---|
| GENRE | | RATING | ★ ★ ★ ★ ★ |
| NOTES | | | |

| MOVIE TITLE | | DATE WATCHED | |
|---|---|---|---|
| GENRE | | RATING | ★ ★ ★ ★ ★ |
| NOTES | | | |

| MOVIE TITLE | | DATE WATCHED | |
|---|---|---|---|
| GENRE | | RATING | ★ ★ ★ ★ ★ |
| NOTES | | | |

| MOVIE TITLE | | DATE WATCHED | |
|---|---|---|---|
| GENRE | | RATING | ★ ★ ★ ★ ★ |
| NOTES | | | |

| MOVIE TITLE | | DATE WATCHED | |
|---|---|---|---|
| GENRE | | RATING | ★ ★ ★ ★ ★ |
| NOTES | | | |

| MOVIE TITLE | | DATE WATCHED | |
|---|---|---|---|
| GENRE | | RATING | ★ ★ ★ ★ ★ |
| NOTES | | | |

| MOVIE TITLE | | DATE WATCHED | |
|---|---|---|---|
| GENRE | | RATING | ★ ★ ★ ★ ★ |
| NOTES | | | |

# My Movie Tracker

| MOVIE TITLE | | DATE WATCHED | |
|---|---|---|---|
| GENRE | | RATING | ☆ ☆ ☆ ☆ ☆ |
| NOTES | | | |

| MOVIE TITLE | | DATE WATCHED | |
|---|---|---|---|
| GENRE | | RATING | ☆ ☆ ☆ ☆ ☆ |
| NOTES | | | |

| MOVIE TITLE | | DATE WATCHED | |
|---|---|---|---|
| GENRE | | RATING | ☆ ☆ ☆ ☆ ☆ |
| NOTES | | | |

| MOVIE TITLE | | DATE WATCHED | |
|---|---|---|---|
| GENRE | | RATING | ☆ ☆ ☆ ☆ ☆ |
| NOTES | | | |

| MOVIE TITLE | | DATE WATCHED | |
|---|---|---|---|
| GENRE | | RATING | ☆ ☆ ☆ ☆ ☆ |
| NOTES | | | |

| MOVIE TITLE | | DATE WATCHED | |
|---|---|---|---|
| GENRE | | RATING | ☆ ☆ ☆ ☆ ☆ |
| NOTES | | | |

| MOVIE TITLE | | DATE WATCHED | |
|---|---|---|---|
| GENRE | | RATING | ☆ ☆ ☆ ☆ ☆ |
| NOTES | | | |

| MOVIE TITLE | | DATE WATCHED | |
|---|---|---|---|
| GENRE | | RATING | ☆ ☆ ☆ ☆ ☆ |
| NOTES | | | |

# My Movie Tracker

| MOVIE TITLE | | DATE WATCHED | |
|---|---|---|---|
| GENRE | | RATING | ☆ ☆ ☆ ☆ ☆ |
| NOTES | | | |

| MOVIE TITLE | | DATE WATCHED | |
|---|---|---|---|
| GENRE | | RATING | ☆ ☆ ☆ ☆ ☆ |
| NOTES | | | |

| MOVIE TITLE | | DATE WATCHED | |
|---|---|---|---|
| GENRE | | RATING | ☆ ☆ ☆ ☆ ☆ |
| NOTES | | | |

| MOVIE TITLE | | DATE WATCHED | |
|---|---|---|---|
| GENRE | | RATING | ☆ ☆ ☆ ☆ ☆ |
| NOTES | | | |

| MOVIE TITLE | | DATE WATCHED | |
|---|---|---|---|
| GENRE | | RATING | ☆ ☆ ☆ ☆ ☆ |
| NOTES | | | |

| MOVIE TITLE | | DATE WATCHED | |
|---|---|---|---|
| GENRE | | RATING | ☆ ☆ ☆ ☆ ☆ |
| NOTES | | | |

| MOVIE TITLE | | DATE WATCHED | |
|---|---|---|---|
| GENRE | | RATING | ☆ ☆ ☆ ☆ ☆ |
| NOTES | | | |

| MOVIE TITLE | | DATE WATCHED | |
|---|---|---|---|
| GENRE | | RATING | ☆ ☆ ☆ ☆ ☆ |
| NOTES | | | |

# My Movie Tracker

| MOVIE TITLE | | DATE WATCHED | |
|---|---|---|---|
| GENRE | | RATING | ☆ ☆ ☆ ☆ ☆ |
| NOTES | | | |

| MOVIE TITLE | | DATE WATCHED | |
|---|---|---|---|
| GENRE | | RATING | ☆ ☆ ☆ ☆ ☆ |
| NOTES | | | |

| MOVIE TITLE | | DATE WATCHED | |
|---|---|---|---|
| GENRE | | RATING | ☆ ☆ ☆ ☆ ☆ |
| NOTES | | | |

| MOVIE TITLE | | DATE WATCHED | |
|---|---|---|---|
| GENRE | | RATING | ☆ ☆ ☆ ☆ ☆ |
| NOTES | | | |

| MOVIE TITLE | | DATE WATCHED | |
|---|---|---|---|
| GENRE | | RATING | ☆ ☆ ☆ ☆ ☆ |
| NOTES | | | |

| MOVIE TITLE | | DATE WATCHED | |
|---|---|---|---|
| GENRE | | RATING | ☆ ☆ ☆ ☆ ☆ |
| NOTES | | | |

| MOVIE TITLE | | DATE WATCHED | |
|---|---|---|---|
| GENRE | | RATING | ☆ ☆ ☆ ☆ ☆ |
| NOTES | | | |

| MOVIE TITLE | | DATE WATCHED | |
|---|---|---|---|
| GENRE | | RATING | ☆ ☆ ☆ ☆ ☆ |
| NOTES | | | |

# My Movie Tracker

| MOVIE TITLE | | DATE WATCHED | |
|---|---|---|---|
| GENRE | | RATING | ☆☆☆☆☆ |
| NOTES | | | |

| MOVIE TITLE | | DATE WATCHED | |
|---|---|---|---|
| GENRE | | RATING | ☆☆☆☆☆ |
| NOTES | | | |

| MOVIE TITLE | | DATE WATCHED | |
|---|---|---|---|
| GENRE | | RATING | ☆☆☆☆☆ |
| NOTES | | | |

| MOVIE TITLE | | DATE WATCHED | |
|---|---|---|---|
| GENRE | | RATING | ☆☆☆☆☆ |
| NOTES | | | |

| MOVIE TITLE | | DATE WATCHED | |
|---|---|---|---|
| GENRE | | RATING | ☆☆☆☆☆ |
| NOTES | | | |

| MOVIE TITLE | | DATE WATCHED | |
|---|---|---|---|
| GENRE | | RATING | ☆☆☆☆☆ |
| NOTES | | | |

| MOVIE TITLE | | DATE WATCHED | |
|---|---|---|---|
| GENRE | | RATING | ☆☆☆☆☆ |
| NOTES | | | |

| MOVIE TITLE | | DATE WATCHED | |
|---|---|---|---|
| GENRE | | RATING | ☆☆☆☆☆ |
| NOTES | | | |

# My Movie Tracker

| MOVIE TITLE | | DATE WATCHED | |
|---|---|---|---|
| GENRE | | RATING | ☆ ☆ ☆ ☆ ☆ |
| NOTES | | | |

| MOVIE TITLE | | DATE WATCHED | |
|---|---|---|---|
| GENRE | | RATING | ☆ ☆ ☆ ☆ ☆ |
| NOTES | | | |

| MOVIE TITLE | | DATE WATCHED | |
|---|---|---|---|
| GENRE | | RATING | ☆ ☆ ☆ ☆ ☆ |
| NOTES | | | |

| MOVIE TITLE | | DATE WATCHED | |
|---|---|---|---|
| GENRE | | RATING | ☆ ☆ ☆ ☆ ☆ |
| NOTES | | | |

| MOVIE TITLE | | DATE WATCHED | |
|---|---|---|---|
| GENRE | | RATING | ☆ ☆ ☆ ☆ ☆ |
| NOTES | | | |

| MOVIE TITLE | | DATE WATCHED | |
|---|---|---|---|
| GENRE | | RATING | ☆ ☆ ☆ ☆ ☆ |
| NOTES | | | |

| MOVIE TITLE | | DATE WATCHED | |
|---|---|---|---|
| GENRE | | RATING | ☆ ☆ ☆ ☆ ☆ |
| NOTES | | | |

| MOVIE TITLE | | DATE WATCHED | |
|---|---|---|---|
| GENRE | | RATING | ☆ ☆ ☆ ☆ ☆ |
| NOTES | | | |

# My Movie Tracker

| MOVIE TITLE | | DATE WATCHED | |
|---|---|---|---|
| GENRE | | RATING | ☆ ☆ ☆ ☆ ☆ |
| NOTES | | | |

| MOVIE TITLE | | DATE WATCHED | |
|---|---|---|---|
| GENRE | | RATING | ☆ ☆ ☆ ☆ ☆ |
| NOTES | | | |

| MOVIE TITLE | | DATE WATCHED | |
|---|---|---|---|
| GENRE | | RATING | ☆ ☆ ☆ ☆ ☆ |
| NOTES | | | |

| MOVIE TITLE | | DATE WATCHED | |
|---|---|---|---|
| GENRE | | RATING | ☆ ☆ ☆ ☆ ☆ |
| NOTES | | | |

| MOVIE TITLE | | DATE WATCHED | |
|---|---|---|---|
| GENRE | | RATING | ☆ ☆ ☆ ☆ ☆ |
| NOTES | | | |

| MOVIE TITLE | | DATE WATCHED | |
|---|---|---|---|
| GENRE | | RATING | ☆ ☆ ☆ ☆ ☆ |
| NOTES | | | |

| MOVIE TITLE | | DATE WATCHED | |
|---|---|---|---|
| GENRE | | RATING | ☆ ☆ ☆ ☆ ☆ |
| NOTES | | | |

| MOVIE TITLE | | DATE WATCHED | |
|---|---|---|---|
| GENRE | | RATING | ☆ ☆ ☆ ☆ ☆ |
| NOTES | | | |

# My Movie Tracker

| MOVIE TITLE | | DATE WATCHED | |
|---|---|---|---|
| GENRE | | RATING | ☆ ☆ ☆ ☆ ☆ |
| NOTES | | | |

| MOVIE TITLE | | DATE WATCHED | |
|---|---|---|---|
| GENRE | | RATING | ☆ ☆ ☆ ☆ ☆ |
| NOTES | | | |

| MOVIE TITLE | | DATE WATCHED | |
|---|---|---|---|
| GENRE | | RATING | ☆ ☆ ☆ ☆ ☆ |
| NOTES | | | |

| MOVIE TITLE | | DATE WATCHED | |
|---|---|---|---|
| GENRE | | RATING | ☆ ☆ ☆ ☆ ☆ |
| NOTES | | | |

| MOVIE TITLE | | DATE WATCHED | |
|---|---|---|---|
| GENRE | | RATING | ☆ ☆ ☆ ☆ ☆ |
| NOTES | | | |

| MOVIE TITLE | | DATE WATCHED | |
|---|---|---|---|
| GENRE | | RATING | ☆ ☆ ☆ ☆ ☆ |
| NOTES | | | |

| MOVIE TITLE | | DATE WATCHED | |
|---|---|---|---|
| GENRE | | RATING | ☆ ☆ ☆ ☆ ☆ |
| NOTES | | | |

| MOVIE TITLE | | DATE WATCHED | |
|---|---|---|---|
| GENRE | | RATING | ☆ ☆ ☆ ☆ ☆ |
| NOTES | | | |

# My Movie Tracker

| MOVIE TITLE | | DATE WATCHED | |
|---|---|---|---|
| GENRE | | RATING | ☆☆☆☆☆ |
| NOTES | | | |

| MOVIE TITLE | | DATE WATCHED | |
|---|---|---|---|
| GENRE | | RATING | ☆☆☆☆☆ |
| NOTES | | | |

| MOVIE TITLE | | DATE WATCHED | |
|---|---|---|---|
| GENRE | | RATING | ☆☆☆☆☆ |
| NOTES | | | |

| MOVIE TITLE | | DATE WATCHED | |
|---|---|---|---|
| GENRE | | RATING | ☆☆☆☆☆ |
| NOTES | | | |

| MOVIE TITLE | | DATE WATCHED | |
|---|---|---|---|
| GENRE | | RATING | ☆☆☆☆☆ |
| NOTES | | | |

| MOVIE TITLE | | DATE WATCHED | |
|---|---|---|---|
| GENRE | | RATING | ☆☆☆☆☆ |
| NOTES | | | |

| MOVIE TITLE | | DATE WATCHED | |
|---|---|---|---|
| GENRE | | RATING | ☆☆☆☆☆ |
| NOTES | | | |

| MOVIE TITLE | | DATE WATCHED | |
|---|---|---|---|
| GENRE | | RATING | ☆☆☆☆☆ |
| NOTES | | | |

# My Movie Tracker

| MOVIE TITLE | | DATE WATCHED | |
|---|---|---|---|
| GENRE | | RATING | ☆ ☆ ☆ ☆ ☆ |
| NOTES | | | |

| MOVIE TITLE | | DATE WATCHED | |
|---|---|---|---|
| GENRE | | RATING | ☆ ☆ ☆ ☆ ☆ |
| NOTES | | | |

| MOVIE TITLE | | DATE WATCHED | |
|---|---|---|---|
| GENRE | | RATING | ☆ ☆ ☆ ☆ ☆ |
| NOTES | | | |

| MOVIE TITLE | | DATE WATCHED | |
|---|---|---|---|
| GENRE | | RATING | ☆ ☆ ☆ ☆ ☆ |
| NOTES | | | |

| MOVIE TITLE | | DATE WATCHED | |
|---|---|---|---|
| GENRE | | RATING | ☆ ☆ ☆ ☆ ☆ |
| NOTES | | | |

| MOVIE TITLE | | DATE WATCHED | |
|---|---|---|---|
| GENRE | | RATING | ☆ ☆ ☆ ☆ ☆ |
| NOTES | | | |

| MOVIE TITLE | | DATE WATCHED | |
|---|---|---|---|
| GENRE | | RATING | ☆ ☆ ☆ ☆ ☆ |
| NOTES | | | |

| MOVIE TITLE | | DATE WATCHED | |
|---|---|---|---|
| GENRE | | RATING | ☆ ☆ ☆ ☆ ☆ |
| NOTES | | | |

# My Movie Tracker

| MOVIE TITLE | | DATE WATCHED | |
|---|---|---|---|
| GENRE | | RATING | ☆ ☆ ☆ ☆ ☆ |
| NOTES | | | |

| MOVIE TITLE | | DATE WATCHED | |
|---|---|---|---|
| GENRE | | RATING | ☆ ☆ ☆ ☆ ☆ |
| NOTES | | | |

| MOVIE TITLE | | DATE WATCHED | |
|---|---|---|---|
| GENRE | | RATING | ☆ ☆ ☆ ☆ ☆ |
| NOTES | | | |

| MOVIE TITLE | | DATE WATCHED | |
|---|---|---|---|
| GENRE | | RATING | ☆ ☆ ☆ ☆ ☆ |
| NOTES | | | |

| MOVIE TITLE | | DATE WATCHED | |
|---|---|---|---|
| GENRE | | RATING | ☆ ☆ ☆ ☆ ☆ |
| NOTES | | | |

| MOVIE TITLE | | DATE WATCHED | |
|---|---|---|---|
| GENRE | | RATING | ☆ ☆ ☆ ☆ ☆ |
| NOTES | | | |

| MOVIE TITLE | | DATE WATCHED | |
|---|---|---|---|
| GENRE | | RATING | ☆ ☆ ☆ ☆ ☆ |
| NOTES | | | |

| MOVIE TITLE | | DATE WATCHED | |
|---|---|---|---|
| GENRE | | RATING | ☆ ☆ ☆ ☆ ☆ |
| NOTES | | | |

# My Movie Tracker

| MOVIE TITLE | | DATE WATCHED | |
|---|---|---|---|
| GENRE | | RATING | ☆ ☆ ☆ ☆ ☆ |
| NOTES | | | |

| MOVIE TITLE | | DATE WATCHED | |
|---|---|---|---|
| GENRE | | RATING | ☆ ☆ ☆ ☆ ☆ |
| NOTES | | | |

| MOVIE TITLE | | DATE WATCHED | |
|---|---|---|---|
| GENRE | | RATING | ☆ ☆ ☆ ☆ ☆ |
| NOTES | | | |

| MOVIE TITLE | | DATE WATCHED | |
|---|---|---|---|
| GENRE | | RATING | ☆ ☆ ☆ ☆ ☆ |
| NOTES | | | |

| MOVIE TITLE | | DATE WATCHED | |
|---|---|---|---|
| GENRE | | RATING | ☆ ☆ ☆ ☆ ☆ |
| NOTES | | | |

| MOVIE TITLE | | DATE WATCHED | |
|---|---|---|---|
| GENRE | | RATING | ☆ ☆ ☆ ☆ ☆ |
| NOTES | | | |

| MOVIE TITLE | | DATE WATCHED | |
|---|---|---|---|
| GENRE | | RATING | ☆ ☆ ☆ ☆ ☆ |
| NOTES | | | |

| MOVIE TITLE | | DATE WATCHED | |
|---|---|---|---|
| GENRE | | RATING | ☆ ☆ ☆ ☆ ☆ |
| NOTES | | | |

# My Movie Tracker

| MOVIE TITLE | | DATE WATCHED | |
|---|---|---|---|
| GENRE | | RATING | ☆☆☆☆☆ |
| NOTES | | | |

| MOVIE TITLE | | DATE WATCHED | |
|---|---|---|---|
| GENRE | | RATING | ☆☆☆☆☆ |
| NOTES | | | |

| MOVIE TITLE | | DATE WATCHED | |
|---|---|---|---|
| GENRE | | RATING | ☆☆☆☆☆ |
| NOTES | | | |

| MOVIE TITLE | | DATE WATCHED | |
|---|---|---|---|
| GENRE | | RATING | ☆☆☆☆☆ |
| NOTES | | | |

| MOVIE TITLE | | DATE WATCHED | |
|---|---|---|---|
| GENRE | | RATING | ☆☆☆☆☆ |
| NOTES | | | |

| MOVIE TITLE | | DATE WATCHED | |
|---|---|---|---|
| GENRE | | RATING | ☆☆☆☆☆ |
| NOTES | | | |

| MOVIE TITLE | | DATE WATCHED | |
|---|---|---|---|
| GENRE | | RATING | ☆☆☆☆☆ |
| NOTES | | | |

| MOVIE TITLE | | DATE WATCHED | |
|---|---|---|---|
| GENRE | | RATING | ☆☆☆☆☆ |
| NOTES | | | |

# My Movie Tracker

| MOVIE TITLE | | DATE WATCHED | |
|---|---|---|---|
| GENRE | | RATING | ☆ ☆ ☆ ☆ ☆ |
| NOTES | | | |

| MOVIE TITLE | | DATE WATCHED | |
|---|---|---|---|
| GENRE | | RATING | ☆ ☆ ☆ ☆ ☆ |
| NOTES | | | |

| MOVIE TITLE | | DATE WATCHED | |
|---|---|---|---|
| GENRE | | RATING | ☆ ☆ ☆ ☆ ☆ |
| NOTES | | | |

| MOVIE TITLE | | DATE WATCHED | |
|---|---|---|---|
| GENRE | | RATING | ☆ ☆ ☆ ☆ ☆ |
| NOTES | | | |

| MOVIE TITLE | | DATE WATCHED | |
|---|---|---|---|
| GENRE | | RATING | ☆ ☆ ☆ ☆ ☆ |
| NOTES | | | |

| MOVIE TITLE | | DATE WATCHED | |
|---|---|---|---|
| GENRE | | RATING | ☆ ☆ ☆ ☆ ☆ |
| NOTES | | | |

| MOVIE TITLE | | DATE WATCHED | |
|---|---|---|---|
| GENRE | | RATING | ☆ ☆ ☆ ☆ ☆ |
| NOTES | | | |

| MOVIE TITLE | | DATE WATCHED | |
|---|---|---|---|
| GENRE | | RATING | ☆ ☆ ☆ ☆ ☆ |
| NOTES | | | |

# My Movie Tracker

| MOVIE TITLE | | DATE WATCHED | |
|---|---|---|---|
| GENRE | | RATING | ☆☆☆☆☆ |
| NOTES | | | |

| MOVIE TITLE | | DATE WATCHED | |
|---|---|---|---|
| GENRE | | RATING | ☆☆☆☆☆ |
| NOTES | | | |

| MOVIE TITLE | | DATE WATCHED | |
|---|---|---|---|
| GENRE | | RATING | ☆☆☆☆☆ |
| NOTES | | | |

| MOVIE TITLE | | DATE WATCHED | |
|---|---|---|---|
| GENRE | | RATING | ☆☆☆☆☆ |
| NOTES | | | |

| MOVIE TITLE | | DATE WATCHED | |
|---|---|---|---|
| GENRE | | RATING | ☆☆☆☆☆ |
| NOTES | | | |

| MOVIE TITLE | | DATE WATCHED | |
|---|---|---|---|
| GENRE | | RATING | ☆☆☆☆☆ |
| NOTES | | | |

| MOVIE TITLE | | DATE WATCHED | |
|---|---|---|---|
| GENRE | | RATING | ☆☆☆☆☆ |
| NOTES | | | |

| MOVIE TITLE | | DATE WATCHED | |
|---|---|---|---|
| GENRE | | RATING | ☆☆☆☆☆ |
| NOTES | | | |

# My Movie Tracker

| MOVIE TITLE | | DATE WATCHED | |
|---|---|---|---|
| GENRE | | RATING | ☆ ☆ ☆ ☆ ☆ |
| NOTES | | | |

| MOVIE TITLE | | DATE WATCHED | |
|---|---|---|---|
| GENRE | | RATING | ☆ ☆ ☆ ☆ ☆ |
| NOTES | | | |

| MOVIE TITLE | | DATE WATCHED | |
|---|---|---|---|
| GENRE | | RATING | ☆ ☆ ☆ ☆ ☆ |
| NOTES | | | |

| MOVIE TITLE | | DATE WATCHED | |
|---|---|---|---|
| GENRE | | RATING | ☆ ☆ ☆ ☆ ☆ |
| NOTES | | | |

| MOVIE TITLE | | DATE WATCHED | |
|---|---|---|---|
| GENRE | | RATING | ☆ ☆ ☆ ☆ ☆ |
| NOTES | | | |

| MOVIE TITLE | | DATE WATCHED | |
|---|---|---|---|
| GENRE | | RATING | ☆ ☆ ☆ ☆ ☆ |
| NOTES | | | |

| MOVIE TITLE | | DATE WATCHED | |
|---|---|---|---|
| GENRE | | RATING | ☆ ☆ ☆ ☆ ☆ |
| NOTES | | | |

| MOVIE TITLE | | DATE WATCHED | |
|---|---|---|---|
| GENRE | | RATING | ☆ ☆ ☆ ☆ ☆ |
| NOTES | | | |

# My Movie Tracker

| MOVIE TITLE | | DATE WATCHED | |
|---|---|---|---|
| GENRE | | RATING | ☆ ☆ ☆ ☆ ☆ |
| NOTES | | | |

| MOVIE TITLE | | DATE WATCHED | |
|---|---|---|---|
| GENRE | | RATING | ☆ ☆ ☆ ☆ ☆ |
| NOTES | | | |

| MOVIE TITLE | | DATE WATCHED | |
|---|---|---|---|
| GENRE | | RATING | ☆ ☆ ☆ ☆ ☆ |
| NOTES | | | |

| MOVIE TITLE | | DATE WATCHED | |
|---|---|---|---|
| GENRE | | RATING | ☆ ☆ ☆ ☆ ☆ |
| NOTES | | | |

| MOVIE TITLE | | DATE WATCHED | |
|---|---|---|---|
| GENRE | | RATING | ☆ ☆ ☆ ☆ ☆ |
| NOTES | | | |

| MOVIE TITLE | | DATE WATCHED | |
|---|---|---|---|
| GENRE | | RATING | ☆ ☆ ☆ ☆ ☆ |
| NOTES | | | |

| MOVIE TITLE | | DATE WATCHED | |
|---|---|---|---|
| GENRE | | RATING | ☆ ☆ ☆ ☆ ☆ |
| NOTES | | | |

| MOVIE TITLE | | DATE WATCHED | |
|---|---|---|---|
| GENRE | | RATING | ☆ ☆ ☆ ☆ ☆ |
| NOTES | | | |

# My Movie Tracker

| MOVIE TITLE | | DATE WATCHED | |
|---|---|---|---|
| GENRE | | RATING | ☆ ☆ ☆ ☆ ☆ |
| NOTES | | | |

| MOVIE TITLE | | DATE WATCHED | |
|---|---|---|---|
| GENRE | | RATING | ☆ ☆ ☆ ☆ ☆ |
| NOTES | | | |

| MOVIE TITLE | | DATE WATCHED | |
|---|---|---|---|
| GENRE | | RATING | ☆ ☆ ☆ ☆ ☆ |
| NOTES | | | |

| MOVIE TITLE | | DATE WATCHED | |
|---|---|---|---|
| GENRE | | RATING | ☆ ☆ ☆ ☆ ☆ |
| NOTES | | | |

| MOVIE TITLE | | DATE WATCHED | |
|---|---|---|---|
| GENRE | | RATING | ☆ ☆ ☆ ☆ ☆ |
| NOTES | | | |

| MOVIE TITLE | | DATE WATCHED | |
|---|---|---|---|
| GENRE | | RATING | ☆ ☆ ☆ ☆ ☆ |
| NOTES | | | |

| MOVIE TITLE | | DATE WATCHED | |
|---|---|---|---|
| GENRE | | RATING | ☆ ☆ ☆ ☆ ☆ |
| NOTES | | | |

| MOVIE TITLE | | DATE WATCHED | |
|---|---|---|---|
| GENRE | | RATING | ☆ ☆ ☆ ☆ ☆ |
| NOTES | | | |

# My Movie Tracker

| MOVIE TITLE | | DATE WATCHED | |
|---|---|---|---|
| GENRE | | RATING | ☆ ☆ ☆ ☆ ☆ |
| NOTES | | | |

| MOVIE TITLE | | DATE WATCHED | |
|---|---|---|---|
| GENRE | | RATING | ☆ ☆ ☆ ☆ ☆ |
| NOTES | | | |

| MOVIE TITLE | | DATE WATCHED | |
|---|---|---|---|
| GENRE | | RATING | ☆ ☆ ☆ ☆ ☆ |
| NOTES | | | |

| MOVIE TITLE | | DATE WATCHED | |
|---|---|---|---|
| GENRE | | RATING | ☆ ☆ ☆ ☆ ☆ |
| NOTES | | | |

| MOVIE TITLE | | DATE WATCHED | |
|---|---|---|---|
| GENRE | | RATING | ☆ ☆ ☆ ☆ ☆ |
| NOTES | | | |

| MOVIE TITLE | | DATE WATCHED | |
|---|---|---|---|
| GENRE | | RATING | ☆ ☆ ☆ ☆ ☆ |
| NOTES | | | |

| MOVIE TITLE | | DATE WATCHED | |
|---|---|---|---|
| GENRE | | RATING | ☆ ☆ ☆ ☆ ☆ |
| NOTES | | | |

| MOVIE TITLE | | DATE WATCHED | |
|---|---|---|---|
| GENRE | | RATING | ☆ ☆ ☆ ☆ ☆ |
| NOTES | | | |

# My Movie Tracker

| MOVIE TITLE | | DATE WATCHED | |
|---|---|---|---|
| GENRE | | RATING | ☆ ☆ ☆ ☆ ☆ |
| NOTES | | | |

| MOVIE TITLE | | DATE WATCHED | |
|---|---|---|---|
| GENRE | | RATING | ☆ ☆ ☆ ☆ ☆ |
| NOTES | | | |

| MOVIE TITLE | | DATE WATCHED | |
|---|---|---|---|
| GENRE | | RATING | ☆ ☆ ☆ ☆ ☆ |
| NOTES | | | |

| MOVIE TITLE | | DATE WATCHED | |
|---|---|---|---|
| GENRE | | RATING | ☆ ☆ ☆ ☆ ☆ |
| NOTES | | | |

| MOVIE TITLE | | DATE WATCHED | |
|---|---|---|---|
| GENRE | | RATING | ☆ ☆ ☆ ☆ ☆ |
| NOTES | | | |

| MOVIE TITLE | | DATE WATCHED | |
|---|---|---|---|
| GENRE | | RATING | ☆ ☆ ☆ ☆ ☆ |
| NOTES | | | |

| MOVIE TITLE | | DATE WATCHED | |
|---|---|---|---|
| GENRE | | RATING | ☆ ☆ ☆ ☆ ☆ |
| NOTES | | | |

| MOVIE TITLE | | DATE WATCHED | |
|---|---|---|---|
| GENRE | | RATING | ☆ ☆ ☆ ☆ ☆ |
| NOTES | | | |

# My Movie Tracker

| MOVIE TITLE | | DATE WATCHED | |
|---|---|---|---|
| GENRE | | RATING | ☆ ☆ ☆ ☆ ☆ |
| NOTES | | | |

| MOVIE TITLE | | DATE WATCHED | |
|---|---|---|---|
| GENRE | | RATING | ☆ ☆ ☆ ☆ ☆ |
| NOTES | | | |

| MOVIE TITLE | | DATE WATCHED | |
|---|---|---|---|
| GENRE | | RATING | ☆ ☆ ☆ ☆ ☆ |
| NOTES | | | |

| MOVIE TITLE | | DATE WATCHED | |
|---|---|---|---|
| GENRE | | RATING | ☆ ☆ ☆ ☆ ☆ |
| NOTES | | | |

| MOVIE TITLE | | DATE WATCHED | |
|---|---|---|---|
| GENRE | | RATING | ☆ ☆ ☆ ☆ ☆ |
| NOTES | | | |

| MOVIE TITLE | | DATE WATCHED | |
|---|---|---|---|
| GENRE | | RATING | ☆ ☆ ☆ ☆ ☆ |
| NOTES | | | |

| MOVIE TITLE | | DATE WATCHED | |
|---|---|---|---|
| GENRE | | RATING | ☆ ☆ ☆ ☆ ☆ |
| NOTES | | | |

| MOVIE TITLE | | DATE WATCHED | |
|---|---|---|---|
| GENRE | | RATING | ☆ ☆ ☆ ☆ ☆ |
| NOTES | | | |

# My Movie Tracker

| MOVIE TITLE | | DATE WATCHED | |
|---|---|---|---|
| GENRE | | RATING | ☆ ☆ ☆ ☆ ☆ |
| NOTES | | | |

| MOVIE TITLE | | DATE WATCHED | |
|---|---|---|---|
| GENRE | | RATING | ☆ ☆ ☆ ☆ ☆ |
| NOTES | | | |

| MOVIE TITLE | | DATE WATCHED | |
|---|---|---|---|
| GENRE | | RATING | ☆ ☆ ☆ ☆ ☆ |
| NOTES | | | |

| MOVIE TITLE | | DATE WATCHED | |
|---|---|---|---|
| GENRE | | RATING | ☆ ☆ ☆ ☆ ☆ |
| NOTES | | | |

| MOVIE TITLE | | DATE WATCHED | |
|---|---|---|---|
| GENRE | | RATING | ☆ ☆ ☆ ☆ ☆ |
| NOTES | | | |

| MOVIE TITLE | | DATE WATCHED | |
|---|---|---|---|
| GENRE | | RATING | ☆ ☆ ☆ ☆ ☆ |
| NOTES | | | |

| MOVIE TITLE | | DATE WATCHED | |
|---|---|---|---|
| GENRE | | RATING | ☆ ☆ ☆ ☆ ☆ |
| NOTES | | | |

| MOVIE TITLE | | DATE WATCHED | |
|---|---|---|---|
| GENRE | | RATING | ☆ ☆ ☆ ☆ ☆ |
| NOTES | | | |

# My Movie Tracker

| MOVIE TITLE | | DATE WATCHED | |
|---|---|---|---|
| GENRE | | RATING | ☆☆☆☆☆ |
| NOTES | | | |

| MOVIE TITLE | | DATE WATCHED | |
|---|---|---|---|
| GENRE | | RATING | ☆☆☆☆☆ |
| NOTES | | | |

| MOVIE TITLE | | DATE WATCHED | |
|---|---|---|---|
| GENRE | | RATING | ☆☆☆☆☆ |
| NOTES | | | |

| MOVIE TITLE | | DATE WATCHED | |
|---|---|---|---|
| GENRE | | RATING | ☆☆☆☆☆ |
| NOTES | | | |

| MOVIE TITLE | | DATE WATCHED | |
|---|---|---|---|
| GENRE | | RATING | ☆☆☆☆☆ |
| NOTES | | | |

| MOVIE TITLE | | DATE WATCHED | |
|---|---|---|---|
| GENRE | | RATING | ☆☆☆☆☆ |
| NOTES | | | |

| MOVIE TITLE | | DATE WATCHED | |
|---|---|---|---|
| GENRE | | RATING | ☆☆☆☆☆ |
| NOTES | | | |

| MOVIE TITLE | | DATE WATCHED | |
|---|---|---|---|
| GENRE | | RATING | ☆☆☆☆☆ |
| NOTES | | | |

# My Movie Tracker

| MOVIE TITLE | | DATE WATCHED | |
|---|---|---|---|
| GENRE | | RATING | ☆ ☆ ☆ ☆ ☆ |
| NOTES | | | |

| MOVIE TITLE | | DATE WATCHED | |
|---|---|---|---|
| GENRE | | RATING | ☆ ☆ ☆ ☆ ☆ |
| NOTES | | | |

| MOVIE TITLE | | DATE WATCHED | |
|---|---|---|---|
| GENRE | | RATING | ☆ ☆ ☆ ☆ ☆ |
| NOTES | | | |

| MOVIE TITLE | | DATE WATCHED | |
|---|---|---|---|
| GENRE | | RATING | ☆ ☆ ☆ ☆ ☆ |
| NOTES | | | |

| MOVIE TITLE | | DATE WATCHED | |
|---|---|---|---|
| GENRE | | RATING | ☆ ☆ ☆ ☆ ☆ |
| NOTES | | | |

| MOVIE TITLE | | DATE WATCHED | |
|---|---|---|---|
| GENRE | | RATING | ☆ ☆ ☆ ☆ ☆ |
| NOTES | | | |

| MOVIE TITLE | | DATE WATCHED | |
|---|---|---|---|
| GENRE | | RATING | ☆ ☆ ☆ ☆ ☆ |
| NOTES | | | |

| MOVIE TITLE | | DATE WATCHED | |
|---|---|---|---|
| GENRE | | RATING | ☆ ☆ ☆ ☆ ☆ |
| NOTES | | | |

# My Movie Tracker

| MOVIE TITLE | | DATE WATCHED | |
|---|---|---|---|
| GENRE | | RATING | ☆ ☆ ☆ ☆ ☆ |
| NOTES | | | |

| MOVIE TITLE | | DATE WATCHED | |
|---|---|---|---|
| GENRE | | RATING | ☆ ☆ ☆ ☆ ☆ |
| NOTES | | | |

| MOVIE TITLE | | DATE WATCHED | |
|---|---|---|---|
| GENRE | | RATING | ☆ ☆ ☆ ☆ ☆ |
| NOTES | | | |

| MOVIE TITLE | | DATE WATCHED | |
|---|---|---|---|
| GENRE | | RATING | ☆ ☆ ☆ ☆ ☆ |
| NOTES | | | |

| MOVIE TITLE | | DATE WATCHED | |
|---|---|---|---|
| GENRE | | RATING | ☆ ☆ ☆ ☆ ☆ |
| NOTES | | | |

| MOVIE TITLE | | DATE WATCHED | |
|---|---|---|---|
| GENRE | | RATING | ☆ ☆ ☆ ☆ ☆ |
| NOTES | | | |

| MOVIE TITLE | | DATE WATCHED | |
|---|---|---|---|
| GENRE | | RATING | ☆ ☆ ☆ ☆ ☆ |
| NOTES | | | |

| MOVIE TITLE | | DATE WATCHED | |
|---|---|---|---|
| GENRE | | RATING | ☆ ☆ ☆ ☆ ☆ |
| NOTES | | | |

# My Movie Tracker

| MOVIE TITLE | | DATE WATCHED | |
|---|---|---|---|
| GENRE | | RATING | ☆ ☆ ☆ ☆ ☆ |
| NOTES | | | |

| MOVIE TITLE | | DATE WATCHED | |
|---|---|---|---|
| GENRE | | RATING | ☆ ☆ ☆ ☆ ☆ |
| NOTES | | | |

| MOVIE TITLE | | DATE WATCHED | |
|---|---|---|---|
| GENRE | | RATING | ☆ ☆ ☆ ☆ ☆ |
| NOTES | | | |

| MOVIE TITLE | | DATE WATCHED | |
|---|---|---|---|
| GENRE | | RATING | ☆ ☆ ☆ ☆ ☆ |
| NOTES | | | |

| MOVIE TITLE | | DATE WATCHED | |
|---|---|---|---|
| GENRE | | RATING | ☆ ☆ ☆ ☆ ☆ |
| NOTES | | | |

| MOVIE TITLE | | DATE WATCHED | |
|---|---|---|---|
| GENRE | | RATING | ☆ ☆ ☆ ☆ ☆ |
| NOTES | | | |

| MOVIE TITLE | | DATE WATCHED | |
|---|---|---|---|
| GENRE | | RATING | ☆ ☆ ☆ ☆ ☆ |
| NOTES | | | |

| MOVIE TITLE | | DATE WATCHED | |
|---|---|---|---|
| GENRE | | RATING | ☆ ☆ ☆ ☆ ☆ |
| NOTES | | | |

# My Movie Tracker

| MOVIE TITLE | | DATE WATCHED | |
|---|---|---|---|
| GENRE | | RATING | ☆☆☆☆☆ |
| NOTES | | | |

| MOVIE TITLE | | DATE WATCHED | |
|---|---|---|---|
| GENRE | | RATING | ☆☆☆☆☆ |
| NOTES | | | |

| MOVIE TITLE | | DATE WATCHED | |
|---|---|---|---|
| GENRE | | RATING | ☆☆☆☆☆ |
| NOTES | | | |

| MOVIE TITLE | | DATE WATCHED | |
|---|---|---|---|
| GENRE | | RATING | ☆☆☆☆☆ |
| NOTES | | | |

| MOVIE TITLE | | DATE WATCHED | |
|---|---|---|---|
| GENRE | | RATING | ☆☆☆☆☆ |
| NOTES | | | |

| MOVIE TITLE | | DATE WATCHED | |
|---|---|---|---|
| GENRE | | RATING | ☆☆☆☆☆ |
| NOTES | | | |

| MOVIE TITLE | | DATE WATCHED | |
|---|---|---|---|
| GENRE | | RATING | ☆☆☆☆☆ |
| NOTES | | | |

| MOVIE TITLE | | DATE WATCHED | |
|---|---|---|---|
| GENRE | | RATING | ☆☆☆☆☆ |
| NOTES | | | |

# My Movie Tracker

| MOVIE TITLE | | DATE WATCHED | |
|---|---|---|---|
| GENRE | | RATING | ☆ ☆ ☆ ☆ ☆ |
| NOTES | | | |

| MOVIE TITLE | | DATE WATCHED | |
|---|---|---|---|
| GENRE | | RATING | ☆ ☆ ☆ ☆ ☆ |
| NOTES | | | |

| MOVIE TITLE | | DATE WATCHED | |
|---|---|---|---|
| GENRE | | RATING | ☆ ☆ ☆ ☆ ☆ |
| NOTES | | | |

| MOVIE TITLE | | DATE WATCHED | |
|---|---|---|---|
| GENRE | | RATING | ☆ ☆ ☆ ☆ ☆ |
| NOTES | | | |

| MOVIE TITLE | | DATE WATCHED | |
|---|---|---|---|
| GENRE | | RATING | ☆ ☆ ☆ ☆ ☆ |
| NOTES | | | |

| MOVIE TITLE | | DATE WATCHED | |
|---|---|---|---|
| GENRE | | RATING | ☆ ☆ ☆ ☆ ☆ |
| NOTES | | | |

| MOVIE TITLE | | DATE WATCHED | |
|---|---|---|---|
| GENRE | | RATING | ☆ ☆ ☆ ☆ ☆ |
| NOTES | | | |

| MOVIE TITLE | | DATE WATCHED | |
|---|---|---|---|
| GENRE | | RATING | ☆ ☆ ☆ ☆ ☆ |
| NOTES | | | |

# My Movie Tracker

| MOVIE TITLE | | DATE WATCHED | |
|---|---|---|---|
| GENRE | | RATING | ☆ ☆ ☆ ☆ ☆ |
| NOTES | | | |

| MOVIE TITLE | | DATE WATCHED | |
|---|---|---|---|
| GENRE | | RATING | ☆ ☆ ☆ ☆ ☆ |
| NOTES | | | |

| MOVIE TITLE | | DATE WATCHED | |
|---|---|---|---|
| GENRE | | RATING | ☆ ☆ ☆ ☆ ☆ |
| NOTES | | | |

| MOVIE TITLE | | DATE WATCHED | |
|---|---|---|---|
| GENRE | | RATING | ☆ ☆ ☆ ☆ ☆ |
| NOTES | | | |

| MOVIE TITLE | | DATE WATCHED | |
|---|---|---|---|
| GENRE | | RATING | ☆ ☆ ☆ ☆ ☆ |
| NOTES | | | |

| MOVIE TITLE | | DATE WATCHED | |
|---|---|---|---|
| GENRE | | RATING | ☆ ☆ ☆ ☆ ☆ |
| NOTES | | | |

| MOVIE TITLE | | DATE WATCHED | |
|---|---|---|---|
| GENRE | | RATING | ☆ ☆ ☆ ☆ ☆ |
| NOTES | | | |

| MOVIE TITLE | | DATE WATCHED | |
|---|---|---|---|
| GENRE | | RATING | ☆ ☆ ☆ ☆ ☆ |
| NOTES | | | |

# My Movie Tracker

| MOVIE TITLE | | DATE WATCHED | |
|---|---|---|---|
| GENRE | | RATING | ☆ ☆ ☆ ☆ ☆ |
| NOTES | | | |

| MOVIE TITLE | | DATE WATCHED | |
|---|---|---|---|
| GENRE | | RATING | ☆ ☆ ☆ ☆ ☆ |
| NOTES | | | |

| MOVIE TITLE | | DATE WATCHED | |
|---|---|---|---|
| GENRE | | RATING | ☆ ☆ ☆ ☆ ☆ |
| NOTES | | | |

| MOVIE TITLE | | DATE WATCHED | |
|---|---|---|---|
| GENRE | | RATING | ☆ ☆ ☆ ☆ ☆ |
| NOTES | | | |

| MOVIE TITLE | | DATE WATCHED | |
|---|---|---|---|
| GENRE | | RATING | ☆ ☆ ☆ ☆ ☆ |
| NOTES | | | |

| MOVIE TITLE | | DATE WATCHED | |
|---|---|---|---|
| GENRE | | RATING | ☆ ☆ ☆ ☆ ☆ |
| NOTES | | | |

| MOVIE TITLE | | DATE WATCHED | |
|---|---|---|---|
| GENRE | | RATING | ☆ ☆ ☆ ☆ ☆ |
| NOTES | | | |

| MOVIE TITLE | | DATE WATCHED | |
|---|---|---|---|
| GENRE | | RATING | ☆ ☆ ☆ ☆ ☆ |
| NOTES | | | |

# My Movie Tracker

| MOVIE TITLE | | DATE WATCHED | |
|---|---|---|---|
| GENRE | | RATING | ☆ ☆ ☆ ☆ ☆ |
| NOTES | | | |

| MOVIE TITLE | | DATE WATCHED | |
|---|---|---|---|
| GENRE | | RATING | ☆ ☆ ☆ ☆ ☆ |
| NOTES | | | |

| MOVIE TITLE | | DATE WATCHED | |
|---|---|---|---|
| GENRE | | RATING | ☆ ☆ ☆ ☆ ☆ |
| NOTES | | | |

| MOVIE TITLE | | DATE WATCHED | |
|---|---|---|---|
| GENRE | | RATING | ☆ ☆ ☆ ☆ ☆ |
| NOTES | | | |

| MOVIE TITLE | | DATE WATCHED | |
|---|---|---|---|
| GENRE | | RATING | ☆ ☆ ☆ ☆ ☆ |
| NOTES | | | |

| MOVIE TITLE | | DATE WATCHED | |
|---|---|---|---|
| GENRE | | RATING | ☆ ☆ ☆ ☆ ☆ |
| NOTES | | | |

| MOVIE TITLE | | DATE WATCHED | |
|---|---|---|---|
| GENRE | | RATING | ☆ ☆ ☆ ☆ ☆ |
| NOTES | | | |

| MOVIE TITLE | | DATE WATCHED | |
|---|---|---|---|
| GENRE | | RATING | ☆ ☆ ☆ ☆ ☆ |
| NOTES | | | |

# My Movie Tracker

| MOVIE TITLE | | DATE WATCHED | |
|---|---|---|---|
| GENRE | | RATING | ☆ ☆ ☆ ☆ ☆ |
| NOTES | | | |

| MOVIE TITLE | | DATE WATCHED | |
|---|---|---|---|
| GENRE | | RATING | ☆ ☆ ☆ ☆ ☆ |
| NOTES | | | |

| MOVIE TITLE | | DATE WATCHED | |
|---|---|---|---|
| GENRE | | RATING | ☆ ☆ ☆ ☆ ☆ |
| NOTES | | | |

| MOVIE TITLE | | DATE WATCHED | |
|---|---|---|---|
| GENRE | | RATING | ☆ ☆ ☆ ☆ ☆ |
| NOTES | | | |

| MOVIE TITLE | | DATE WATCHED | |
|---|---|---|---|
| GENRE | | RATING | ☆ ☆ ☆ ☆ ☆ |
| NOTES | | | |

| MOVIE TITLE | | DATE WATCHED | |
|---|---|---|---|
| GENRE | | RATING | ☆ ☆ ☆ ☆ ☆ |
| NOTES | | | |

| MOVIE TITLE | | DATE WATCHED | |
|---|---|---|---|
| GENRE | | RATING | ☆ ☆ ☆ ☆ ☆ |
| NOTES | | | |

| MOVIE TITLE | | DATE WATCHED | |
|---|---|---|---|
| GENRE | | RATING | ☆ ☆ ☆ ☆ ☆ |
| NOTES | | | |

# My Movie Tracker

| MOVIE TITLE | | DATE WATCHED | |
|---|---|---|---|
| GENRE | | RATING | ☆ ☆ ☆ ☆ ☆ |
| NOTES | | | |

| MOVIE TITLE | | DATE WATCHED | |
|---|---|---|---|
| GENRE | | RATING | ☆ ☆ ☆ ☆ ☆ |
| NOTES | | | |

| MOVIE TITLE | | DATE WATCHED | |
|---|---|---|---|
| GENRE | | RATING | ☆ ☆ ☆ ☆ ☆ |
| NOTES | | | |

| MOVIE TITLE | | DATE WATCHED | |
|---|---|---|---|
| GENRE | | RATING | ☆ ☆ ☆ ☆ ☆ |
| NOTES | | | |

| MOVIE TITLE | | DATE WATCHED | |
|---|---|---|---|
| GENRE | | RATING | ☆ ☆ ☆ ☆ ☆ |
| NOTES | | | |

| MOVIE TITLE | | DATE WATCHED | |
|---|---|---|---|
| GENRE | | RATING | ☆ ☆ ☆ ☆ ☆ |
| NOTES | | | |

| MOVIE TITLE | | DATE WATCHED | |
|---|---|---|---|
| GENRE | | RATING | ☆ ☆ ☆ ☆ ☆ |
| NOTES | | | |

| MOVIE TITLE | | DATE WATCHED | |
|---|---|---|---|
| GENRE | | RATING | ☆ ☆ ☆ ☆ ☆ |
| NOTES | | | |

# My Movie Tracker

| MOVIE TITLE | | DATE WATCHED | |
|---|---|---|---|
| GENRE | | RATING | ☆ ☆ ☆ ☆ ☆ |
| NOTES | | | |

| MOVIE TITLE | | DATE WATCHED | |
|---|---|---|---|
| GENRE | | RATING | ☆ ☆ ☆ ☆ ☆ |
| NOTES | | | |

| MOVIE TITLE | | DATE WATCHED | |
|---|---|---|---|
| GENRE | | RATING | ☆ ☆ ☆ ☆ ☆ |
| NOTES | | | |

| MOVIE TITLE | | DATE WATCHED | |
|---|---|---|---|
| GENRE | | RATING | ☆ ☆ ☆ ☆ ☆ |
| NOTES | | | |

| MOVIE TITLE | | DATE WATCHED | |
|---|---|---|---|
| GENRE | | RATING | ☆ ☆ ☆ ☆ ☆ |
| NOTES | | | |

| MOVIE TITLE | | DATE WATCHED | |
|---|---|---|---|
| GENRE | | RATING | ☆ ☆ ☆ ☆ ☆ |
| NOTES | | | |

| MOVIE TITLE | | DATE WATCHED | |
|---|---|---|---|
| GENRE | | RATING | ☆ ☆ ☆ ☆ ☆ |
| NOTES | | | |

| MOVIE TITLE | | DATE WATCHED | |
|---|---|---|---|
| GENRE | | RATING | ☆ ☆ ☆ ☆ ☆ |
| NOTES | | | |

# My Movie Tracker

| MOVIE TITLE | | DATE WATCHED | |
|---|---|---|---|
| GENRE | | RATING | ☆ ☆ ☆ ☆ ☆ |
| NOTES | | | |

| MOVIE TITLE | | DATE WATCHED | |
|---|---|---|---|
| GENRE | | RATING | ☆ ☆ ☆ ☆ ☆ |
| NOTES | | | |

| MOVIE TITLE | | DATE WATCHED | |
|---|---|---|---|
| GENRE | | RATING | ☆ ☆ ☆ ☆ ☆ |
| NOTES | | | |

| MOVIE TITLE | | DATE WATCHED | |
|---|---|---|---|
| GENRE | | RATING | ☆ ☆ ☆ ☆ ☆ |
| NOTES | | | |

| MOVIE TITLE | | DATE WATCHED | |
|---|---|---|---|
| GENRE | | RATING | ☆ ☆ ☆ ☆ ☆ |
| NOTES | | | |

| MOVIE TITLE | | DATE WATCHED | |
|---|---|---|---|
| GENRE | | RATING | ☆ ☆ ☆ ☆ ☆ |
| NOTES | | | |

| MOVIE TITLE | | DATE WATCHED | |
|---|---|---|---|
| GENRE | | RATING | ☆ ☆ ☆ ☆ ☆ |
| NOTES | | | |

| MOVIE TITLE | | DATE WATCHED | |
|---|---|---|---|
| GENRE | | RATING | ☆ ☆ ☆ ☆ ☆ |
| NOTES | | | |

# My Movie Tracker

| MOVIE TITLE | | DATE WATCHED | |
|---|---|---|---|
| GENRE | | RATING | ☆ ☆ ☆ ☆ ☆ |
| NOTES | | | |

| MOVIE TITLE | | DATE WATCHED | |
|---|---|---|---|
| GENRE | | RATING | ☆ ☆ ☆ ☆ ☆ |
| NOTES | | | |

| MOVIE TITLE | | DATE WATCHED | |
|---|---|---|---|
| GENRE | | RATING | ☆ ☆ ☆ ☆ ☆ |
| NOTES | | | |

| MOVIE TITLE | | DATE WATCHED | |
|---|---|---|---|
| GENRE | | RATING | ☆ ☆ ☆ ☆ ☆ |
| NOTES | | | |

| MOVIE TITLE | | DATE WATCHED | |
|---|---|---|---|
| GENRE | | RATING | ☆ ☆ ☆ ☆ ☆ |
| NOTES | | | |

| MOVIE TITLE | | DATE WATCHED | |
|---|---|---|---|
| GENRE | | RATING | ☆ ☆ ☆ ☆ ☆ |
| NOTES | | | |

| MOVIE TITLE | | DATE WATCHED | |
|---|---|---|---|
| GENRE | | RATING | ☆ ☆ ☆ ☆ ☆ |
| NOTES | | | |

| MOVIE TITLE | | DATE WATCHED | |
|---|---|---|---|
| GENRE | | RATING | ☆ ☆ ☆ ☆ ☆ |
| NOTES | | | |

# My Movie Tracker

| MOVIE TITLE | | DATE WATCHED | |
|---|---|---|---|
| GENRE | | RATING | ☆ ☆ ☆ ☆ ☆ |
| NOTES | | | |

| MOVIE TITLE | | DATE WATCHED | |
|---|---|---|---|
| GENRE | | RATING | ☆ ☆ ☆ ☆ ☆ |
| NOTES | | | |

| MOVIE TITLE | | DATE WATCHED | |
|---|---|---|---|
| GENRE | | RATING | ☆ ☆ ☆ ☆ ☆ |
| NOTES | | | |

| MOVIE TITLE | | DATE WATCHED | |
|---|---|---|---|
| GENRE | | RATING | ☆ ☆ ☆ ☆ ☆ |
| NOTES | | | |

| MOVIE TITLE | | DATE WATCHED | |
|---|---|---|---|
| GENRE | | RATING | ☆ ☆ ☆ ☆ ☆ |
| NOTES | | | |

| MOVIE TITLE | | DATE WATCHED | |
|---|---|---|---|
| GENRE | | RATING | ☆ ☆ ☆ ☆ ☆ |
| NOTES | | | |

| MOVIE TITLE | | DATE WATCHED | |
|---|---|---|---|
| GENRE | | RATING | ☆ ☆ ☆ ☆ ☆ |
| NOTES | | | |

| MOVIE TITLE | | DATE WATCHED | |
|---|---|---|---|
| GENRE | | RATING | ☆ ☆ ☆ ☆ ☆ |
| NOTES | | | |

# My Movie Tracker

| MOVIE TITLE | | DATE WATCHED | |
|---|---|---|---|
| GENRE | | RATING | ☆ ☆ ☆ ☆ ☆ |
| NOTES | | | |

| MOVIE TITLE | | DATE WATCHED | |
|---|---|---|---|
| GENRE | | RATING | ☆ ☆ ☆ ☆ ☆ |
| NOTES | | | |

| MOVIE TITLE | | DATE WATCHED | |
|---|---|---|---|
| GENRE | | RATING | ☆ ☆ ☆ ☆ ☆ |
| NOTES | | | |

| MOVIE TITLE | | DATE WATCHED | |
|---|---|---|---|
| GENRE | | RATING | ☆ ☆ ☆ ☆ ☆ |
| NOTES | | | |

| MOVIE TITLE | | DATE WATCHED | |
|---|---|---|---|
| GENRE | | RATING | ☆ ☆ ☆ ☆ ☆ |
| NOTES | | | |

| MOVIE TITLE | | DATE WATCHED | |
|---|---|---|---|
| GENRE | | RATING | ☆ ☆ ☆ ☆ ☆ |
| NOTES | | | |

| MOVIE TITLE | | DATE WATCHED | |
|---|---|---|---|
| GENRE | | RATING | ☆ ☆ ☆ ☆ ☆ |
| NOTES | | | |

| MOVIE TITLE | | DATE WATCHED | |
|---|---|---|---|
| GENRE | | RATING | ☆ ☆ ☆ ☆ ☆ |
| NOTES | | | |

# My Movie Tracker

| MOVIE TITLE | | DATE WATCHED | |
|---|---|---|---|
| GENRE | | RATING | ☆ ☆ ☆ ☆ ☆ |
| NOTES | | | |

| MOVIE TITLE | | DATE WATCHED | |
|---|---|---|---|
| GENRE | | RATING | ☆ ☆ ☆ ☆ ☆ |
| NOTES | | | |

| MOVIE TITLE | | DATE WATCHED | |
|---|---|---|---|
| GENRE | | RATING | ☆ ☆ ☆ ☆ ☆ |
| NOTES | | | |

| MOVIE TITLE | | DATE WATCHED | |
|---|---|---|---|
| GENRE | | RATING | ☆ ☆ ☆ ☆ ☆ |
| NOTES | | | |

| MOVIE TITLE | | DATE WATCHED | |
|---|---|---|---|
| GENRE | | RATING | ☆ ☆ ☆ ☆ ☆ |
| NOTES | | | |

| MOVIE TITLE | | DATE WATCHED | |
|---|---|---|---|
| GENRE | | RATING | ☆ ☆ ☆ ☆ ☆ |
| NOTES | | | |

| MOVIE TITLE | | DATE WATCHED | |
|---|---|---|---|
| GENRE | | RATING | ☆ ☆ ☆ ☆ ☆ |
| NOTES | | | |

| MOVIE TITLE | | DATE WATCHED | |
|---|---|---|---|
| GENRE | | RATING | ☆ ☆ ☆ ☆ ☆ |
| NOTES | | | |

# My Movie Tracker

| MOVIE TITLE | | DATE WATCHED | |
|---|---|---|---|
| GENRE | | RATING | ☆ ☆ ☆ ☆ ☆ |
| NOTES | | | |

| MOVIE TITLE | | DATE WATCHED | |
|---|---|---|---|
| GENRE | | RATING | ☆ ☆ ☆ ☆ ☆ |
| NOTES | | | |

| MOVIE TITLE | | DATE WATCHED | |
|---|---|---|---|
| GENRE | | RATING | ☆ ☆ ☆ ☆ ☆ |
| NOTES | | | |

| MOVIE TITLE | | DATE WATCHED | |
|---|---|---|---|
| GENRE | | RATING | ☆ ☆ ☆ ☆ ☆ |
| NOTES | | | |

| MOVIE TITLE | | DATE WATCHED | |
|---|---|---|---|
| GENRE | | RATING | ☆ ☆ ☆ ☆ ☆ |
| NOTES | | | |

| MOVIE TITLE | | DATE WATCHED | |
|---|---|---|---|
| GENRE | | RATING | ☆ ☆ ☆ ☆ ☆ |
| NOTES | | | |

| MOVIE TITLE | | DATE WATCHED | |
|---|---|---|---|
| GENRE | | RATING | ☆ ☆ ☆ ☆ ☆ |
| NOTES | | | |

| MOVIE TITLE | | DATE WATCHED | |
|---|---|---|---|
| GENRE | | RATING | ☆ ☆ ☆ ☆ ☆ |
| NOTES | | | |

# My Movie Tracker

| MOVIE TITLE | | DATE WATCHED | |
|---|---|---|---|
| GENRE | | RATING | ☆ ☆ ☆ ☆ ☆ |
| NOTES | | | |

| MOVIE TITLE | | DATE WATCHED | |
|---|---|---|---|
| GENRE | | RATING | ☆ ☆ ☆ ☆ ☆ |
| NOTES | | | |

| MOVIE TITLE | | DATE WATCHED | |
|---|---|---|---|
| GENRE | | RATING | ☆ ☆ ☆ ☆ ☆ |
| NOTES | | | |

| MOVIE TITLE | | DATE WATCHED | |
|---|---|---|---|
| GENRE | | RATING | ☆ ☆ ☆ ☆ ☆ |
| NOTES | | | |

| MOVIE TITLE | | DATE WATCHED | |
|---|---|---|---|
| GENRE | | RATING | ☆ ☆ ☆ ☆ ☆ |
| NOTES | | | |

| MOVIE TITLE | | DATE WATCHED | |
|---|---|---|---|
| GENRE | | RATING | ☆ ☆ ☆ ☆ ☆ |
| NOTES | | | |

| MOVIE TITLE | | DATE WATCHED | |
|---|---|---|---|
| GENRE | | RATING | ☆ ☆ ☆ ☆ ☆ |
| NOTES | | | |

| MOVIE TITLE | | DATE WATCHED | |
|---|---|---|---|
| GENRE | | RATING | ☆ ☆ ☆ ☆ ☆ |
| NOTES | | | |

# My Movie Tracker

| MOVIE TITLE | | DATE WATCHED | |
|---|---|---|---|
| GENRE | | RATING | ☆ ☆ ☆ ☆ ☆ |
| NOTES | | | |

| MOVIE TITLE | | DATE WATCHED | |
|---|---|---|---|
| GENRE | | RATING | ☆ ☆ ☆ ☆ ☆ |
| NOTES | | | |

| MOVIE TITLE | | DATE WATCHED | |
|---|---|---|---|
| GENRE | | RATING | ☆ ☆ ☆ ☆ ☆ |
| NOTES | | | |

| MOVIE TITLE | | DATE WATCHED | |
|---|---|---|---|
| GENRE | | RATING | ☆ ☆ ☆ ☆ ☆ |
| NOTES | | | |

| MOVIE TITLE | | DATE WATCHED | |
|---|---|---|---|
| GENRE | | RATING | ☆ ☆ ☆ ☆ ☆ |
| NOTES | | | |

| MOVIE TITLE | | DATE WATCHED | |
|---|---|---|---|
| GENRE | | RATING | ☆ ☆ ☆ ☆ ☆ |
| NOTES | | | |

| MOVIE TITLE | | DATE WATCHED | |
|---|---|---|---|
| GENRE | | RATING | ☆ ☆ ☆ ☆ ☆ |
| NOTES | | | |

| MOVIE TITLE | | DATE WATCHED | |
|---|---|---|---|
| GENRE | | RATING | ☆ ☆ ☆ ☆ ☆ |
| NOTES | | | |

# My Movie Tracker

| MOVIE TITLE | | DATE WATCHED | |
|---|---|---|---|
| GENRE | | RATING | ☆ ☆ ☆ ☆ ☆ |
| NOTES | | | |

| MOVIE TITLE | | DATE WATCHED | |
|---|---|---|---|
| GENRE | | RATING | ☆ ☆ ☆ ☆ ☆ |
| NOTES | | | |

| MOVIE TITLE | | DATE WATCHED | |
|---|---|---|---|
| GENRE | | RATING | ☆ ☆ ☆ ☆ ☆ |
| NOTES | | | |

| MOVIE TITLE | | DATE WATCHED | |
|---|---|---|---|
| GENRE | | RATING | ☆ ☆ ☆ ☆ ☆ |
| NOTES | | | |

| MOVIE TITLE | | DATE WATCHED | |
|---|---|---|---|
| GENRE | | RATING | ☆ ☆ ☆ ☆ ☆ |
| NOTES | | | |

| MOVIE TITLE | | DATE WATCHED | |
|---|---|---|---|
| GENRE | | RATING | ☆ ☆ ☆ ☆ ☆ |
| NOTES | | | |

| MOVIE TITLE | | DATE WATCHED | |
|---|---|---|---|
| GENRE | | RATING | ☆ ☆ ☆ ☆ ☆ |
| NOTES | | | |

| MOVIE TITLE | | DATE WATCHED | |
|---|---|---|---|
| GENRE | | RATING | ☆ ☆ ☆ ☆ ☆ |
| NOTES | | | |

# My Movie Tracker

| MOVIE TITLE | | DATE WATCHED | |
|---|---|---|---|
| GENRE | | RATING | ☆ ☆ ☆ ☆ ☆ |
| NOTES | | | |

| MOVIE TITLE | | DATE WATCHED | |
|---|---|---|---|
| GENRE | | RATING | ☆ ☆ ☆ ☆ ☆ |
| NOTES | | | |

| MOVIE TITLE | | DATE WATCHED | |
|---|---|---|---|
| GENRE | | RATING | ☆ ☆ ☆ ☆ ☆ |
| NOTES | | | |

| MOVIE TITLE | | DATE WATCHED | |
|---|---|---|---|
| GENRE | | RATING | ☆ ☆ ☆ ☆ ☆ |
| NOTES | | | |

| MOVIE TITLE | | DATE WATCHED | |
|---|---|---|---|
| GENRE | | RATING | ☆ ☆ ☆ ☆ ☆ |
| NOTES | | | |

| MOVIE TITLE | | DATE WATCHED | |
|---|---|---|---|
| GENRE | | RATING | ☆ ☆ ☆ ☆ ☆ |
| NOTES | | | |

| MOVIE TITLE | | DATE WATCHED | |
|---|---|---|---|
| GENRE | | RATING | ☆ ☆ ☆ ☆ ☆ |
| NOTES | | | |

| MOVIE TITLE | | DATE WATCHED | |
|---|---|---|---|
| GENRE | | RATING | ☆ ☆ ☆ ☆ ☆ |
| NOTES | | | |

# My Movie Tracker

| MOVIE TITLE | | DATE WATCHED | |
|---|---|---|---|
| GENRE | | RATING | ☆ ☆ ☆ ☆ ☆ |
| NOTES | | | |

| MOVIE TITLE | | DATE WATCHED | |
|---|---|---|---|
| GENRE | | RATING | ☆ ☆ ☆ ☆ ☆ |
| NOTES | | | |

| MOVIE TITLE | | DATE WATCHED | |
|---|---|---|---|
| GENRE | | RATING | ☆ ☆ ☆ ☆ ☆ |
| NOTES | | | |

| MOVIE TITLE | | DATE WATCHED | |
|---|---|---|---|
| GENRE | | RATING | ☆ ☆ ☆ ☆ ☆ |
| NOTES | | | |

| MOVIE TITLE | | DATE WATCHED | |
|---|---|---|---|
| GENRE | | RATING | ☆ ☆ ☆ ☆ ☆ |
| NOTES | | | |

| MOVIE TITLE | | DATE WATCHED | |
|---|---|---|---|
| GENRE | | RATING | ☆ ☆ ☆ ☆ ☆ |
| NOTES | | | |

| MOVIE TITLE | | DATE WATCHED | |
|---|---|---|---|
| GENRE | | RATING | ☆ ☆ ☆ ☆ ☆ |
| NOTES | | | |

| MOVIE TITLE | | DATE WATCHED | |
|---|---|---|---|
| GENRE | | RATING | ☆ ☆ ☆ ☆ ☆ |
| NOTES | | | |

# My Movie Tracker

| MOVIE TITLE | | DATE WATCHED | |
|---|---|---|---|
| GENRE | | RATING | ☆ ☆ ☆ ☆ ☆ |
| NOTES | | | |

| MOVIE TITLE | | DATE WATCHED | |
|---|---|---|---|
| GENRE | | RATING | ☆ ☆ ☆ ☆ ☆ |
| NOTES | | | |

| MOVIE TITLE | | DATE WATCHED | |
|---|---|---|---|
| GENRE | | RATING | ☆ ☆ ☆ ☆ ☆ |
| NOTES | | | |

| MOVIE TITLE | | DATE WATCHED | |
|---|---|---|---|
| GENRE | | RATING | ☆ ☆ ☆ ☆ ☆ |
| NOTES | | | |

| MOVIE TITLE | | DATE WATCHED | |
|---|---|---|---|
| GENRE | | RATING | ☆ ☆ ☆ ☆ ☆ |
| NOTES | | | |

| MOVIE TITLE | | DATE WATCHED | |
|---|---|---|---|
| GENRE | | RATING | ☆ ☆ ☆ ☆ ☆ |
| NOTES | | | |

| MOVIE TITLE | | DATE WATCHED | |
|---|---|---|---|
| GENRE | | RATING | ☆ ☆ ☆ ☆ ☆ |
| NOTES | | | |

| MOVIE TITLE | | DATE WATCHED | |
|---|---|---|---|
| GENRE | | RATING | ☆ ☆ ☆ ☆ ☆ |
| NOTES | | | |

# My Movie Tracker

| MOVIE TITLE | | DATE WATCHED | |
|---|---|---|---|
| GENRE | | RATING | ☆ ☆ ☆ ☆ ☆ |
| NOTES | | | |

| MOVIE TITLE | | DATE WATCHED | |
|---|---|---|---|
| GENRE | | RATING | ☆ ☆ ☆ ☆ ☆ |
| NOTES | | | |

| MOVIE TITLE | | DATE WATCHED | |
|---|---|---|---|
| GENRE | | RATING | ☆ ☆ ☆ ☆ ☆ |
| NOTES | | | |

| MOVIE TITLE | | DATE WATCHED | |
|---|---|---|---|
| GENRE | | RATING | ☆ ☆ ☆ ☆ ☆ |
| NOTES | | | |

| MOVIE TITLE | | DATE WATCHED | |
|---|---|---|---|
| GENRE | | RATING | ☆ ☆ ☆ ☆ ☆ |
| NOTES | | | |

| MOVIE TITLE | | DATE WATCHED | |
|---|---|---|---|
| GENRE | | RATING | ☆ ☆ ☆ ☆ ☆ |
| NOTES | | | |

| MOVIE TITLE | | DATE WATCHED | |
|---|---|---|---|
| GENRE | | RATING | ☆ ☆ ☆ ☆ ☆ |
| NOTES | | | |

| MOVIE TITLE | | DATE WATCHED | |
|---|---|---|---|
| GENRE | | RATING | ☆ ☆ ☆ ☆ ☆ |
| NOTES | | | |

# My Movie Tracker

| MOVIE TITLE | | DATE WATCHED | |
|---|---|---|---|
| GENRE | | RATING | ☆ ☆ ☆ ☆ ☆ |
| NOTES | | | |

| MOVIE TITLE | | DATE WATCHED | |
|---|---|---|---|
| GENRE | | RATING | ☆ ☆ ☆ ☆ ☆ |
| NOTES | | | |

| MOVIE TITLE | | DATE WATCHED | |
|---|---|---|---|
| GENRE | | RATING | ☆ ☆ ☆ ☆ ☆ |
| NOTES | | | |

| MOVIE TITLE | | DATE WATCHED | |
|---|---|---|---|
| GENRE | | RATING | ☆ ☆ ☆ ☆ ☆ |
| NOTES | | | |

| MOVIE TITLE | | DATE WATCHED | |
|---|---|---|---|
| GENRE | | RATING | ☆ ☆ ☆ ☆ ☆ |
| NOTES | | | |

| MOVIE TITLE | | DATE WATCHED | |
|---|---|---|---|
| GENRE | | RATING | ☆ ☆ ☆ ☆ ☆ |
| NOTES | | | |

| MOVIE TITLE | | DATE WATCHED | |
|---|---|---|---|
| GENRE | | RATING | ☆ ☆ ☆ ☆ ☆ |
| NOTES | | | |

| MOVIE TITLE | | DATE WATCHED | |
|---|---|---|---|
| GENRE | | RATING | ☆ ☆ ☆ ☆ ☆ |
| NOTES | | | |

# My Movie Tracker

| MOVIE TITLE | | DATE WATCHED | |
|---|---|---|---|
| GENRE | | RATING | ☆ ☆ ☆ ☆ ☆ |
| NOTES | | | |

| MOVIE TITLE | | DATE WATCHED | |
|---|---|---|---|
| GENRE | | RATING | ☆ ☆ ☆ ☆ ☆ |
| NOTES | | | |

| MOVIE TITLE | | DATE WATCHED | |
|---|---|---|---|
| GENRE | | RATING | ☆ ☆ ☆ ☆ ☆ |
| NOTES | | | |

| MOVIE TITLE | | DATE WATCHED | |
|---|---|---|---|
| GENRE | | RATING | ☆ ☆ ☆ ☆ ☆ |
| NOTES | | | |

| MOVIE TITLE | | DATE WATCHED | |
|---|---|---|---|
| GENRE | | RATING | ☆ ☆ ☆ ☆ ☆ |
| NOTES | | | |

| MOVIE TITLE | | DATE WATCHED | |
|---|---|---|---|
| GENRE | | RATING | ☆ ☆ ☆ ☆ ☆ |
| NOTES | | | |

| MOVIE TITLE | | DATE WATCHED | |
|---|---|---|---|
| GENRE | | RATING | ☆ ☆ ☆ ☆ ☆ |
| NOTES | | | |

| MOVIE TITLE | | DATE WATCHED | |
|---|---|---|---|
| GENRE | | RATING | ☆ ☆ ☆ ☆ ☆ |
| NOTES | | | |

# My Movie Tracker

| MOVIE TITLE | | DATE WATCHED | |
|---|---|---|---|
| GENRE | | RATING | ☆ ☆ ☆ ☆ ☆ |
| NOTES | | | |

| MOVIE TITLE | | DATE WATCHED | |
|---|---|---|---|
| GENRE | | RATING | ☆ ☆ ☆ ☆ ☆ |
| NOTES | | | |

| MOVIE TITLE | | DATE WATCHED | |
|---|---|---|---|
| GENRE | | RATING | ☆ ☆ ☆ ☆ ☆ |
| NOTES | | | |

| MOVIE TITLE | | DATE WATCHED | |
|---|---|---|---|
| GENRE | | RATING | ☆ ☆ ☆ ☆ ☆ |
| NOTES | | | |

| MOVIE TITLE | | DATE WATCHED | |
|---|---|---|---|
| GENRE | | RATING | ☆ ☆ ☆ ☆ ☆ |
| NOTES | | | |

| MOVIE TITLE | | DATE WATCHED | |
|---|---|---|---|
| GENRE | | RATING | ☆ ☆ ☆ ☆ ☆ |
| NOTES | | | |

| MOVIE TITLE | | DATE WATCHED | |
|---|---|---|---|
| GENRE | | RATING | ☆ ☆ ☆ ☆ ☆ |
| NOTES | | | |

| MOVIE TITLE | | DATE WATCHED | |
|---|---|---|---|
| GENRE | | RATING | ☆ ☆ ☆ ☆ ☆ |
| NOTES | | | |

# My Movie Tracker

| MOVIE TITLE | | DATE WATCHED | |
|---|---|---|---|
| GENRE | | RATING | ☆☆☆☆☆ |
| NOTES | | | |

| MOVIE TITLE | | DATE WATCHED | |
|---|---|---|---|
| GENRE | | RATING | ☆☆☆☆☆ |
| NOTES | | | |

| MOVIE TITLE | | DATE WATCHED | |
|---|---|---|---|
| GENRE | | RATING | ☆☆☆☆☆ |
| NOTES | | | |

| MOVIE TITLE | | DATE WATCHED | |
|---|---|---|---|
| GENRE | | RATING | ☆☆☆☆☆ |
| NOTES | | | |

| MOVIE TITLE | | DATE WATCHED | |
|---|---|---|---|
| GENRE | | RATING | ☆☆☆☆☆ |
| NOTES | | | |

| MOVIE TITLE | | DATE WATCHED | |
|---|---|---|---|
| GENRE | | RATING | ☆☆☆☆☆ |
| NOTES | | | |

| MOVIE TITLE | | DATE WATCHED | |
|---|---|---|---|
| GENRE | | RATING | ☆☆☆☆☆ |
| NOTES | | | |

| MOVIE TITLE | | DATE WATCHED | |
|---|---|---|---|
| GENRE | | RATING | ☆☆☆☆☆ |
| NOTES | | | |

# My Movie Tracker

| MOVIE TITLE | | DATE WATCHED | |
|---|---|---|---|
| GENRE | | RATING | ☆ ☆ ☆ ☆ ☆ |
| NOTES | | | |

| MOVIE TITLE | | DATE WATCHED | |
|---|---|---|---|
| GENRE | | RATING | ☆ ☆ ☆ ☆ ☆ |
| NOTES | | | |

| MOVIE TITLE | | DATE WATCHED | |
|---|---|---|---|
| GENRE | | RATING | ☆ ☆ ☆ ☆ ☆ |
| NOTES | | | |

| MOVIE TITLE | | DATE WATCHED | |
|---|---|---|---|
| GENRE | | RATING | ☆ ☆ ☆ ☆ ☆ |
| NOTES | | | |

| MOVIE TITLE | | DATE WATCHED | |
|---|---|---|---|
| GENRE | | RATING | ☆ ☆ ☆ ☆ ☆ |
| NOTES | | | |

| MOVIE TITLE | | DATE WATCHED | |
|---|---|---|---|
| GENRE | | RATING | ☆ ☆ ☆ ☆ ☆ |
| NOTES | | | |

| MOVIE TITLE | | DATE WATCHED | |
|---|---|---|---|
| GENRE | | RATING | ☆ ☆ ☆ ☆ ☆ |
| NOTES | | | |

| MOVIE TITLE | | DATE WATCHED | |
|---|---|---|---|
| GENRE | | RATING | ☆ ☆ ☆ ☆ ☆ |
| NOTES | | | |

# My Movie Tracker

| MOVIE TITLE | | DATE WATCHED | |
|---|---|---|---|
| GENRE | | RATING | ☆ ☆ ☆ ☆ ☆ |
| NOTES | | | |

| MOVIE TITLE | | DATE WATCHED | |
|---|---|---|---|
| GENRE | | RATING | ☆ ☆ ☆ ☆ ☆ |
| NOTES | | | |

| MOVIE TITLE | | DATE WATCHED | |
|---|---|---|---|
| GENRE | | RATING | ☆ ☆ ☆ ☆ ☆ |
| NOTES | | | |

| MOVIE TITLE | | DATE WATCHED | |
|---|---|---|---|
| GENRE | | RATING | ☆ ☆ ☆ ☆ ☆ |
| NOTES | | | |

| MOVIE TITLE | | DATE WATCHED | |
|---|---|---|---|
| GENRE | | RATING | ☆ ☆ ☆ ☆ ☆ |
| NOTES | | | |

| MOVIE TITLE | | DATE WATCHED | |
|---|---|---|---|
| GENRE | | RATING | ☆ ☆ ☆ ☆ ☆ |
| NOTES | | | |

| MOVIE TITLE | | DATE WATCHED | |
|---|---|---|---|
| GENRE | | RATING | ☆ ☆ ☆ ☆ |
| NOTES | | | |

| MOVIE TITLE | | DATE WATCHED | |
|---|---|---|---|
| GENRE | | RATING | ☆ ☆ ☆ ☆ |
| NOTES | | | |

# My Movie Tracker

| MOVIE TITLE | | DATE WATCHED | |
|---|---|---|---|
| GENRE | | RATING | ☆ ☆ ☆ ☆ ☆ |
| NOTES | | | |

| MOVIE TITLE | | DATE WATCHED | |
|---|---|---|---|
| GENRE | | RATING | ☆ ☆ ☆ ☆ ☆ |
| NOTES | | | |

| MOVIE TITLE | | DATE WATCHED | |
|---|---|---|---|
| GENRE | | RATING | ☆ ☆ ☆ ☆ ☆ |
| NOTES | | | |

| MOVIE TITLE | | DATE WATCHED | |
|---|---|---|---|
| GENRE | | RATING | ☆ ☆ ☆ ☆ ☆ |
| NOTES | | | |

| MOVIE TITLE | | DATE WATCHED | |
|---|---|---|---|
| GENRE | | RATING | ☆ ☆ ☆ ☆ ☆ |
| NOTES | | | |

| MOVIE TITLE | | DATE WATCHED | |
|---|---|---|---|
| GENRE | | RATING | ☆ ☆ ☆ ☆ ☆ |
| NOTES | | | |

| MOVIE TITLE | | DATE WATCHED | |
|---|---|---|---|
| GENRE | | RATING | ☆ ☆ ☆ ☆ ☆ |
| NOTES | | | |

| MOVIE TITLE | | DATE WATCHED | |
|---|---|---|---|
| GENRE | | RATING | ☆ ☆ ☆ ☆ ☆ |
| NOTES | | | |

# My Movie Tracker

| MOVIE TITLE | | DATE WATCHED | |
|---|---|---|---|
| GENRE | | RATING | ☆ ☆ ☆ ☆ ☆ |
| NOTES | | | |

| MOVIE TITLE | | DATE WATCHED | |
|---|---|---|---|
| GENRE | | RATING | ☆ ☆ ☆ ☆ ☆ |
| NOTES | | | |

| MOVIE TITLE | | DATE WATCHED | |
|---|---|---|---|
| GENRE | | RATING | ☆ ☆ ☆ ☆ ☆ |
| NOTES | | | |

| MOVIE TITLE | | DATE WATCHED | |
|---|---|---|---|
| GENRE | | RATING | ☆ ☆ ☆ ☆ ☆ |
| NOTES | | | |

| MOVIE TITLE | | DATE WATCHED | |
|---|---|---|---|
| GENRE | | RATING | ☆ ☆ ☆ ☆ ☆ |
| NOTES | | | |

| MOVIE TITLE | | DATE WATCHED | |
|---|---|---|---|
| GENRE | | RATING | ☆ ☆ ☆ ☆ ☆ |
| NOTES | | | |

| MOVIE TITLE | | DATE WATCHED | |
|---|---|---|---|
| GENRE | | RATING | ☆ ☆ ☆ ☆ ☆ |
| NOTES | | | |

| MOVIE TITLE | | DATE WATCHED | |
|---|---|---|---|
| GENRE | | RATING | ☆ ☆ ☆ ☆ ☆ |
| NOTES | | | |

# My Movie Tracker

| MOVIE TITLE | | DATE WATCHED | |
|---|---|---|---|
| GENRE | | RATING | ☆ ☆ ☆ ☆ ☆ |
| NOTES | | | |

| MOVIE TITLE | | DATE WATCHED | |
|---|---|---|---|
| GENRE | | RATING | ☆ ☆ ☆ ☆ ☆ |
| NOTES | | | |

| MOVIE TITLE | | DATE WATCHED | |
|---|---|---|---|
| GENRE | | RATING | ☆ ☆ ☆ ☆ ☆ |
| NOTES | | | |

| MOVIE TITLE | | DATE WATCHED | |
|---|---|---|---|
| GENRE | | RATING | ☆ ☆ ☆ ☆ ☆ |
| NOTES | | | |

| MOVIE TITLE | | DATE WATCHED | |
|---|---|---|---|
| GENRE | | RATING | ☆ ☆ ☆ ☆ ☆ |
| NOTES | | | |

| MOVIE TITLE | | DATE WATCHED | |
|---|---|---|---|
| GENRE | | RATING | ☆ ☆ ☆ ☆ ☆ |
| NOTES | | | |

| MOVIE TITLE | | DATE WATCHED | |
|---|---|---|---|
| GENRE | | RATING | ☆ ☆ ☆ ☆ ☆ |
| NOTES | | | |

| MOVIE TITLE | | DATE WATCHED | |
|---|---|---|---|
| GENRE | | RATING | ☆ ☆ ☆ ☆ ☆ |
| NOTES | | | |

# My Movie Tracker

| MOVIE TITLE | | DATE WATCHED | |
|---|---|---|---|
| GENRE | | RATING | ☆ ☆ ☆ ☆ ☆ |
| NOTES | | | |

| MOVIE TITLE | | DATE WATCHED | |
|---|---|---|---|
| GENRE | | RATING | ☆ ☆ ☆ ☆ ☆ |
| NOTES | | | |

| MOVIE TITLE | | DATE WATCHED | |
|---|---|---|---|
| GENRE | | RATING | ☆ ☆ ☆ ☆ ☆ |
| NOTES | | | |

| MOVIE TITLE | | DATE WATCHED | |
|---|---|---|---|
| GENRE | | RATING | ☆ ☆ ☆ ☆ ☆ |
| NOTES | | | |

| MOVIE TITLE | | DATE WATCHED | |
|---|---|---|---|
| GENRE | | RATING | ☆ ☆ ☆ ☆ ☆ |
| NOTES | | | |

| MOVIE TITLE | | DATE WATCHED | |
|---|---|---|---|
| GENRE | | RATING | ☆ ☆ ☆ ☆ ☆ |
| NOTES | | | |

| MOVIE TITLE | | DATE WATCHED | |
|---|---|---|---|
| GENRE | | RATING | ☆ ☆ ☆ ☆ ☆ |
| NOTES | | | |

| MOVIE TITLE | | DATE WATCHED | |
|---|---|---|---|
| GENRE | | RATING | ☆ ☆ ☆ ☆ ☆ |
| NOTES | | | |

# My Movie Tracker

| MOVIE TITLE | | DATE WATCHED | |
|---|---|---|---|
| GENRE | | RATING | ☆ ☆ ☆ ☆ ☆ |
| NOTES | | | |

| MOVIE TITLE | | DATE WATCHED | |
|---|---|---|---|
| GENRE | | RATING | ☆ ☆ ☆ ☆ ☆ |
| NOTES | | | |

| MOVIE TITLE | | DATE WATCHED | |
|---|---|---|---|
| GENRE | | RATING | ☆ ☆ ☆ ☆ ☆ |
| NOTES | | | |

| MOVIE TITLE | | DATE WATCHED | |
|---|---|---|---|
| GENRE | | RATING | ☆ ☆ ☆ ☆ ☆ |
| NOTES | | | |

| MOVIE TITLE | | DATE WATCHED | |
|---|---|---|---|
| GENRE | | RATING | ☆ ☆ ☆ ☆ ☆ |
| NOTES | | | |

| MOVIE TITLE | | DATE WATCHED | |
|---|---|---|---|
| GENRE | | RATING | ☆ ☆ ☆ ☆ ☆ |
| NOTES | | | |

| MOVIE TITLE | | DATE WATCHED | |
|---|---|---|---|
| GENRE | | RATING | ☆ ☆ ☆ ☆ ☆ |
| NOTES | | | |

| MOVIE TITLE | | DATE WATCHED | |
|---|---|---|---|
| GENRE | | RATING | ☆ ☆ ☆ ☆ ☆ |
| NOTES | | | |

# My Movie Tracker

| MOVIE TITLE | | DATE WATCHED | |
|---|---|---|---|
| GENRE | | RATING | ☆ ☆ ☆ ☆ ☆ |
| NOTES | | | |

| MOVIE TITLE | | DATE WATCHED | |
|---|---|---|---|
| GENRE | | RATING | ☆ ☆ ☆ ☆ ☆ |
| NOTES | | | |

| MOVIE TITLE | | DATE WATCHED | |
|---|---|---|---|
| GENRE | | RATING | ☆ ☆ ☆ ☆ ☆ |
| NOTES | | | |

| MOVIE TITLE | | DATE WATCHED | |
|---|---|---|---|
| GENRE | | RATING | ☆ ☆ ☆ ☆ ☆ |
| NOTES | | | |

| MOVIE TITLE | | DATE WATCHED | |
|---|---|---|---|
| GENRE | | RATING | ☆ ☆ ☆ ☆ ☆ |
| NOTES | | | |

| MOVIE TITLE | | DATE WATCHED | |
|---|---|---|---|
| GENRE | | RATING | ☆ ☆ ☆ ☆ ☆ |
| NOTES | | | |

| MOVIE TITLE | | DATE WATCHED | |
|---|---|---|---|
| GENRE | | RATING | ☆ ☆ ☆ ☆ ☆ |
| NOTES | | | |

| MOVIE TITLE | | DATE WATCHED | |
|---|---|---|---|
| GENRE | | RATING | ☆ ☆ ☆ ☆ ☆ |
| NOTES | | | |

# My Movie Tracker

| MOVIE TITLE | | DATE WATCHED | |
|---|---|---|---|
| GENRE | | RATING | ☆ ☆ ☆ ☆ ☆ |
| NOTES | | | |

| MOVIE TITLE | | DATE WATCHED | |
|---|---|---|---|
| GENRE | | RATING | ☆ ☆ ☆ ☆ ☆ |
| NOTES | | | |

| MOVIE TITLE | | DATE WATCHED | |
|---|---|---|---|
| GENRE | | RATING | ☆ ☆ ☆ ☆ ☆ |
| NOTES | | | |

| MOVIE TITLE | | DATE WATCHED | |
|---|---|---|---|
| GENRE | | RATING | ☆ ☆ ☆ ☆ ☆ |
| NOTES | | | |

| MOVIE TITLE | | DATE WATCHED | |
|---|---|---|---|
| GENRE | | RATING | ☆ ☆ ☆ ☆ ☆ |
| NOTES | | | |

| MOVIE TITLE | | DATE WATCHED | |
|---|---|---|---|
| GENRE | | RATING | ☆ ☆ ☆ ☆ ☆ |
| NOTES | | | |

| MOVIE TITLE | | DATE WATCHED | |
|---|---|---|---|
| GENRE | | RATING | ☆ ☆ ☆ ☆ ☆ |
| NOTES | | | |

| MOVIE TITLE | | DATE WATCHED | |
|---|---|---|---|
| GENRE | | RATING | ☆ ☆ ☆ ☆ ☆ |
| NOTES | | | |

# My Movie Tracker

| MOVIE TITLE | | DATE WATCHED | |
|---|---|---|---|
| GENRE | | RATING | ☆ ☆ ☆ ☆ ☆ |
| NOTES | | | |

| MOVIE TITLE | | DATE WATCHED | |
|---|---|---|---|
| GENRE | | RATING | ☆ ☆ ☆ ☆ ☆ |
| NOTES | | | |

| MOVIE TITLE | | DATE WATCHED | |
|---|---|---|---|
| GENRE | | RATING | ☆ ☆ ☆ ☆ ☆ |
| NOTES | | | |

| MOVIE TITLE | | DATE WATCHED | |
|---|---|---|---|
| GENRE | | RATING | ☆ ☆ ☆ ☆ ☆ |
| NOTES | | | |

| MOVIE TITLE | | DATE WATCHED | |
|---|---|---|---|
| GENRE | | RATING | ☆ ☆ ☆ ☆ ☆ |
| NOTES | | | |

| MOVIE TITLE | | DATE WATCHED | |
|---|---|---|---|
| GENRE | | RATING | ☆ ☆ ☆ ☆ ☆ |
| NOTES | | | |

| MOVIE TITLE | | DATE WATCHED | |
|---|---|---|---|
| GENRE | | RATING | ☆ ☆ ☆ ☆ ☆ |
| NOTES | | | |

| MOVIE TITLE | | DATE WATCHED | |
|---|---|---|---|
| GENRE | | RATING | ☆ ☆ ☆ ☆ ☆ |
| NOTES | | | |

# My Movie Tracker

| MOVIE TITLE | | DATE WATCHED | |
|---|---|---|---|
| GENRE | | RATING | ☆ ☆ ☆ ☆ ☆ |
| NOTES | | | |

| MOVIE TITLE | | DATE WATCHED | |
|---|---|---|---|
| GENRE | | RATING | ☆ ☆ ☆ ☆ ☆ |
| NOTES | | | |

| MOVIE TITLE | | DATE WATCHED | |
|---|---|---|---|
| GENRE | | RATING | ☆ ☆ ☆ ☆ ☆ |
| NOTES | | | |

| MOVIE TITLE | | DATE WATCHED | |
|---|---|---|---|
| GENRE | | RATING | ☆ ☆ ☆ ☆ ☆ |
| NOTES | | | |

| MOVIE TITLE | | DATE WATCHED | |
|---|---|---|---|
| GENRE | | RATING | ☆ ☆ ☆ ☆ ☆ |
| NOTES | | | |

| MOVIE TITLE | | DATE WATCHED | |
|---|---|---|---|
| GENRE | | RATING | ☆ ☆ ☆ ☆ ☆ |
| NOTES | | | |

| MOVIE TITLE | | DATE WATCHED | |
|---|---|---|---|
| GENRE | | RATING | ☆ ☆ ☆ ☆ ☆ |
| NOTES | | | |

| MOVIE TITLE | | DATE WATCHED | |
|---|---|---|---|
| GENRE | | RATING | ☆ ☆ ☆ ☆ ☆ |
| NOTES | | | |

# My Movie Tracker

| MOVIE TITLE | | DATE WATCHED | |
|---|---|---|---|
| GENRE | | RATING | ☆ ☆ ☆ ☆ ☆ |
| NOTES | | | |

| MOVIE TITLE | | DATE WATCHED | |
|---|---|---|---|
| GENRE | | RATING | ☆ ☆ ☆ ☆ ☆ |
| NOTES | | | |

| MOVIE TITLE | | DATE WATCHED | |
|---|---|---|---|
| GENRE | | RATING | ☆ ☆ ☆ ☆ ☆ |
| NOTES | | | |

| MOVIE TITLE | | DATE WATCHED | |
|---|---|---|---|
| GENRE | | RATING | ☆ ☆ ☆ ☆ ☆ |
| NOTES | | | |

| MOVIE TITLE | | DATE WATCHED | |
|---|---|---|---|
| GENRE | | RATING | ☆ ☆ ☆ ☆ ☆ |
| NOTES | | | |

| MOVIE TITLE | | DATE WATCHED | |
|---|---|---|---|
| GENRE | | RATING | ☆ ☆ ☆ ☆ ☆ |
| NOTES | | | |

| MOVIE TITLE | | DATE WATCHED | |
|---|---|---|---|
| GENRE | | RATING | ☆ ☆ ☆ ☆ ☆ |
| NOTES | | | |

| MOVIE TITLE | | DATE WATCHED | |
|---|---|---|---|
| GENRE | | RATING | ☆ ☆ ☆ ☆ ☆ |
| NOTES | | | |

# My Movie Tracker

| MOVIE TITLE | | DATE WATCHED | |
|---|---|---|---|
| GENRE | | RATING | ☆ ☆ ☆ ☆ ☆ |
| NOTES | | | |

| MOVIE TITLE | | DATE WATCHED | |
|---|---|---|---|
| GENRE | | RATING | ☆ ☆ ☆ ☆ ☆ |
| NOTES | | | |

| MOVIE TITLE | | DATE WATCHED | |
|---|---|---|---|
| GENRE | | RATING | ☆ ☆ ☆ ☆ ☆ |
| NOTES | | | |

| MOVIE TITLE | | DATE WATCHED | |
|---|---|---|---|
| GENRE | | RATING | ☆ ☆ ☆ ☆ ☆ |
| NOTES | | | |

| MOVIE TITLE | | DATE WATCHED | |
|---|---|---|---|
| GENRE | | RATING | ☆ ☆ ☆ ☆ ☆ |
| NOTES | | | |

| MOVIE TITLE | | DATE WATCHED | |
|---|---|---|---|
| GENRE | | RATING | ☆ ☆ ☆ ☆ ☆ |
| NOTES | | | |

| MOVIE TITLE | | DATE WATCHED | |
|---|---|---|---|
| GENRE | | RATING | ☆ ☆ ☆ ☆ ☆ |
| NOTES | | | |

| MOVIE TITLE | | DATE WATCHED | |
|---|---|---|---|
| GENRE | | RATING | ☆ ☆ ☆ ☆ ☆ |
| NOTES | | | |

# My Movie Tracker

| MOVIE TITLE | | DATE WATCHED | |
|---|---|---|---|
| GENRE | | RATING | ☆ ☆ ☆ ☆ ☆ |
| NOTES | | | |

| MOVIE TITLE | | DATE WATCHED | |
|---|---|---|---|
| GENRE | | RATING | ☆ ☆ ☆ ☆ ☆ |
| NOTES | | | |

| MOVIE TITLE | | DATE WATCHED | |
|---|---|---|---|
| GENRE | | RATING | ☆ ☆ ☆ ☆ ☆ |
| NOTES | | | |

| MOVIE TITLE | | DATE WATCHED | |
|---|---|---|---|
| GENRE | | RATING | ☆ ☆ ☆ ☆ ☆ |
| NOTES | | | |

| MOVIE TITLE | | DATE WATCHED | |
|---|---|---|---|
| GENRE | | RATING | ☆ ☆ ☆ ☆ ☆ |
| NOTES | | | |

| MOVIE TITLE | | DATE WATCHED | |
|---|---|---|---|
| GENRE | | RATING | ☆ ☆ ☆ ☆ ☆ |
| NOTES | | | |

| MOVIE TITLE | | DATE WATCHED | |
|---|---|---|---|
| GENRE | | RATING | ☆ ☆ ☆ ☆ ☆ |
| NOTES | | | |

| MOVIE TITLE | | DATE WATCHED | |
|---|---|---|---|
| GENRE | | RATING | ☆ ☆ ☆ ☆ ☆ |
| NOTES | | | |

# My Movie Tracker

| MOVIE TITLE | | DATE WATCHED | |
|---|---|---|---|
| GENRE | | RATING | ☆ ☆ ☆ ☆ ☆ |
| NOTES | | | |

| MOVIE TITLE | | DATE WATCHED | |
|---|---|---|---|
| GENRE | | RATING | ☆ ☆ ☆ ☆ ☆ |
| NOTES | | | |

| MOVIE TITLE | | DATE WATCHED | |
|---|---|---|---|
| GENRE | | RATING | ☆ ☆ ☆ ☆ ☆ |
| NOTES | | | |

| MOVIE TITLE | | DATE WATCHED | |
|---|---|---|---|
| GENRE | | RATING | ☆ ☆ ☆ ☆ ☆ |
| NOTES | | | |

| MOVIE TITLE | | DATE WATCHED | |
|---|---|---|---|
| GENRE | | RATING | ☆ ☆ ☆ ☆ ☆ |
| NOTES | | | |

| MOVIE TITLE | | DATE WATCHED | |
|---|---|---|---|
| GENRE | | RATING | ☆ ☆ ☆ ☆ ☆ |
| NOTES | | | |

| MOVIE TITLE | | DATE WATCHED | |
|---|---|---|---|
| GENRE | | RATING | ☆ ☆ ☆ ☆ ☆ |
| NOTES | | | |

| MOVIE TITLE | | DATE WATCHED | |
|---|---|---|---|
| GENRE | | RATING | ☆ ☆ ☆ ☆ ☆ |
| NOTES | | | |

# My Movie Tracker

| MOVIE TITLE | | DATE WATCHED | |
|---|---|---|---|
| GENRE | | RATING | ☆ ☆ ☆ ☆ ☆ |
| NOTES | | | |

| MOVIE TITLE | | DATE WATCHED | |
|---|---|---|---|
| GENRE | | RATING | ☆ ☆ ☆ ☆ ☆ |
| NOTES | | | |

| MOVIE TITLE | | DATE WATCHED | |
|---|---|---|---|
| GENRE | | RATING | ☆ ☆ ☆ ☆ ☆ |
| NOTES | | | |

| MOVIE TITLE | | DATE WATCHED | |
|---|---|---|---|
| GENRE | | RATING | ☆ ☆ ☆ ☆ ☆ |
| NOTES | | | |

| MOVIE TITLE | | DATE WATCHED | |
|---|---|---|---|
| GENRE | | RATING | ☆ ☆ ☆ ☆ ☆ |
| NOTES | | | |

| MOVIE TITLE | | DATE WATCHED | |
|---|---|---|---|
| GENRE | | RATING | ☆ ☆ ☆ ☆ ☆ |
| NOTES | | | |

| MOVIE TITLE | | DATE WATCHED | |
|---|---|---|---|
| GENRE | | RATING | ☆ ☆ ☆ ☆ ☆ |
| NOTES | | | |

| MOVIE TITLE | | DATE WATCHED | |
|---|---|---|---|
| GENRE | | RATING | ☆ ☆ ☆ ☆ ☆ |
| NOTES | | | |

# My Movie Tracker

| MOVIE TITLE | | DATE WATCHED | |
|---|---|---|---|
| GENRE | | RATING | ☆ ☆ ☆ ☆ ☆ |
| NOTES | | | |

| MOVIE TITLE | | DATE WATCHED | |
|---|---|---|---|
| GENRE | | RATING | ☆ ☆ ☆ ☆ ☆ |
| NOTES | | | |

| MOVIE TITLE | | DATE WATCHED | |
|---|---|---|---|
| GENRE | | RATING | ☆ ☆ ☆ ☆ ☆ |
| NOTES | | | |

| MOVIE TITLE | | DATE WATCHED | |
|---|---|---|---|
| GENRE | | RATING | ☆ ☆ ☆ ☆ ☆ |
| NOTES | | | |

| MOVIE TITLE | | DATE WATCHED | |
|---|---|---|---|
| GENRE | | RATING | ☆ ☆ ☆ ☆ ☆ |
| NOTES | | | |

| MOVIE TITLE | | DATE WATCHED | |
|---|---|---|---|
| GENRE | | RATING | ☆ ☆ ☆ ☆ ☆ |
| NOTES | | | |

| MOVIE TITLE | | DATE WATCHED | |
|---|---|---|---|
| GENRE | | RATING | ☆ ☆ ☆ ☆ ☆ |
| NOTES | | | |

| MOVIE TITLE | | DATE WATCHED | |
|---|---|---|---|
| GENRE | | RATING | ☆ ☆ ☆ ☆ ☆ |
| NOTES | | | |

# My Movie Tracker

| MOVIE TITLE | | DATE WATCHED | |
|---|---|---|---|
| GENRE | | RATING | ☆ ☆ ☆ ☆ ☆ |
| NOTES | | | |

| MOVIE TITLE | | DATE WATCHED | |
|---|---|---|---|
| GENRE | | RATING | ☆ ☆ ☆ ☆ ☆ |
| NOTES | | | |

| MOVIE TITLE | | DATE WATCHED | |
|---|---|---|---|
| GENRE | | RATING | ☆ ☆ ☆ ☆ ☆ |
| NOTES | | | |

| MOVIE TITLE | | DATE WATCHED | |
|---|---|---|---|
| GENRE | | RATING | ☆ ☆ ☆ ☆ ☆ |
| NOTES | | | |

| MOVIE TITLE | | DATE WATCHED | |
|---|---|---|---|
| GENRE | | RATING | ☆ ☆ ☆ ☆ ☆ |
| NOTES | | | |

| MOVIE TITLE | | DATE WATCHED | |
|---|---|---|---|
| GENRE | | RATING | ☆ ☆ ☆ ☆ ☆ |
| NOTES | | | |

| MOVIE TITLE | | DATE WATCHED | |
|---|---|---|---|
| GENRE | | RATING | ☆ ☆ ☆ ☆ ☆ |
| NOTES | | | |

| MOVIE TITLE | | DATE WATCHED | |
|---|---|---|---|
| GENRE | | RATING | ☆ ☆ ☆ ☆ ☆ |
| NOTES | | | |

# My Movie Tracker

| MOVIE TITLE | | DATE WATCHED | |
|---|---|---|---|
| GENRE | | RATING | ☆ ☆ ☆ ☆ ☆ |
| NOTES | | | |

| MOVIE TITLE | | DATE WATCHED | |
|---|---|---|---|
| GENRE | | RATING | ☆ ☆ ☆ ☆ ☆ |
| NOTES | | | |

| MOVIE TITLE | | DATE WATCHED | |
|---|---|---|---|
| GENRE | | RATING | ☆ ☆ ☆ ☆ ☆ |
| NOTES | | | |

| MOVIE TITLE | | DATE WATCHED | |
|---|---|---|---|
| GENRE | | RATING | ☆ ☆ ☆ ☆ ☆ |
| NOTES | | | |

| MOVIE TITLE | | DATE WATCHED | |
|---|---|---|---|
| GENRE | | RATING | ☆ ☆ ☆ ☆ ☆ |
| NOTES | | | |

| MOVIE TITLE | | DATE WATCHED | |
|---|---|---|---|
| GENRE | | RATING | ☆ ☆ ☆ ☆ ☆ |
| NOTES | | | |

| MOVIE TITLE | | DATE WATCHED | |
|---|---|---|---|
| GENRE | | RATING | ☆ ☆ ☆ ☆ ☆ |
| NOTES | | | |

| MOVIE TITLE | | DATE WATCHED | |
|---|---|---|---|
| GENRE | | RATING | ☆ ☆ ☆ ☆ ☆ |
| NOTES | | | |

# My Movie Tracker

| MOVIE TITLE | | DATE WATCHED | |
|---|---|---|---|
| GENRE | | RATING | ☆ ☆ ☆ ☆ ☆ |
| NOTES | | | |

| MOVIE TITLE | | DATE WATCHED | |
|---|---|---|---|
| GENRE | | RATING | ☆ ☆ ☆ ☆ ☆ |
| NOTES | | | |

| MOVIE TITLE | | DATE WATCHED | |
|---|---|---|---|
| GENRE | | RATING | ☆ ☆ ☆ ☆ ☆ |
| NOTES | | | |

| MOVIE TITLE | | DATE WATCHED | |
|---|---|---|---|
| GENRE | | RATING | ☆ ☆ ☆ ☆ ☆ |
| NOTES | | | |

| MOVIE TITLE | | DATE WATCHED | |
|---|---|---|---|
| GENRE | | RATING | ☆ ☆ ☆ ☆ ☆ |
| NOTES | | | |

| MOVIE TITLE | | DATE WATCHED | |
|---|---|---|---|
| GENRE | | RATING | ☆ ☆ ☆ ☆ ☆ |
| NOTES | | | |

| MOVIE TITLE | | DATE WATCHED | |
|---|---|---|---|
| GENRE | | RATING | ☆ ☆ ☆ ☆ ☆ |
| NOTES | | | |

| MOVIE TITLE | | DATE WATCHED | |
|---|---|---|---|
| GENRE | | RATING | ☆ ☆ ☆ ☆ ☆ |
| NOTES | | | |

# My Movie Tracker

| MOVIE TITLE | | DATE WATCHED | |
|---|---|---|---|
| GENRE | | RATING | ☆ ☆ ☆ ☆ ☆ |
| NOTES | | | |

| MOVIE TITLE | | DATE WATCHED | |
|---|---|---|---|
| GENRE | | RATING | ☆ ☆ ☆ ☆ ☆ |
| NOTES | | | |

| MOVIE TITLE | | DATE WATCHED | |
|---|---|---|---|
| GENRE | | RATING | ☆ ☆ ☆ ☆ ☆ |
| NOTES | | | |

| MOVIE TITLE | | DATE WATCHED | |
|---|---|---|---|
| GENRE | | RATING | ☆ ☆ ☆ ☆ ☆ |
| NOTES | | | |

| MOVIE TITLE | | DATE WATCHED | |
|---|---|---|---|
| GENRE | | RATING | ☆ ☆ ☆ ☆ ☆ |
| NOTES | | | |

| MOVIE TITLE | | DATE WATCHED | |
|---|---|---|---|
| GENRE | | RATING | ☆ ☆ ☆ ☆ ☆ |
| NOTES | | | |

| MOVIE TITLE | | DATE WATCHED | |
|---|---|---|---|
| GENRE | | RATING | ☆ ☆ ☆ ☆ ☆ |
| NOTES | | | |

| MOVIE TITLE | | DATE WATCHED | |
|---|---|---|---|
| GENRE | | RATING | ☆ ☆ ☆ ☆ ☆ |
| NOTES | | | |

# My Movie Tracker

| MOVIE TITLE | | DATE WATCHED | |
|---|---|---|---|
| GENRE | | RATING | ☆ ☆ ☆ ☆ ☆ |
| NOTES | | | |

| MOVIE TITLE | | DATE WATCHED | |
|---|---|---|---|
| GENRE | | RATING | ☆ ☆ ☆ ☆ ☆ |
| NOTES | | | |

| MOVIE TITLE | | DATE WATCHED | |
|---|---|---|---|
| GENRE | | RATING | ☆ ☆ ☆ ☆ ☆ |
| NOTES | | | |

| MOVIE TITLE | | DATE WATCHED | |
|---|---|---|---|
| GENRE | | RATING | ☆ ☆ ☆ ☆ ☆ |
| NOTES | | | |

| MOVIE TITLE | | DATE WATCHED | |
|---|---|---|---|
| GENRE | | RATING | ☆ ☆ ☆ ☆ ☆ |
| NOTES | | | |

| MOVIE TITLE | | DATE WATCHED | |
|---|---|---|---|
| GENRE | | RATING | ☆ ☆ ☆ ☆ ☆ |
| NOTES | | | |

| MOVIE TITLE | | DATE WATCHED | |
|---|---|---|---|
| GENRE | | RATING | ☆ ☆ ☆ ☆ ☆ |
| NOTES | | | |

| MOVIE TITLE | | DATE WATCHED | |
|---|---|---|---|
| GENRE | | RATING | ☆ ☆ ☆ ☆ ☆ |
| NOTES | | | |

# My Movie Tracker

| MOVIE TITLE | | DATE WATCHED | |
|---|---|---|---|
| GENRE | | RATING | ☆ ☆ ☆ ☆ ☆ |
| NOTES | | | |

| MOVIE TITLE | | DATE WATCHED | |
|---|---|---|---|
| GENRE | | RATING | ☆ ☆ ☆ ☆ ☆ |
| NOTES | | | |

| MOVIE TITLE | | DATE WATCHED | |
|---|---|---|---|
| GENRE | | RATING | ☆ ☆ ☆ ☆ ☆ |
| NOTES | | | |

| MOVIE TITLE | | DATE WATCHED | |
|---|---|---|---|
| GENRE | | RATING | ☆ ☆ ☆ ☆ ☆ |
| NOTES | | | |

| MOVIE TITLE | | DATE WATCHED | |
|---|---|---|---|
| GENRE | | RATING | ☆ ☆ ☆ ☆ ☆ |
| NOTES | | | |

| MOVIE TITLE | | DATE WATCHED | |
|---|---|---|---|
| GENRE | | RATING | ☆ ☆ ☆ ☆ ☆ |
| NOTES | | | |

| MOVIE TITLE | | DATE WATCHED | |
|---|---|---|---|
| GENRE | | RATING | ☆ ☆ ☆ ☆ ☆ |
| NOTES | | | |

| MOVIE TITLE | | DATE WATCHED | |
|---|---|---|---|
| GENRE | | RATING | ☆ ☆ ☆ ☆ ☆ |
| NOTES | | | |

# My Movie Tracker

| MOVIE TITLE | | DATE WATCHED | |
|---|---|---|---|
| GENRE | | RATING | ☆ ☆ ☆ ☆ ☆ |
| NOTES | | | |

| MOVIE TITLE | | DATE WATCHED | |
|---|---|---|---|
| GENRE | | RATING | ☆ ☆ ☆ ☆ ☆ |
| NOTES | | | |

| MOVIE TITLE | | DATE WATCHED | |
|---|---|---|---|
| GENRE | | RATING | ☆ ☆ ☆ ☆ ☆ |
| NOTES | | | |

| MOVIE TITLE | | DATE WATCHED | |
|---|---|---|---|
| GENRE | | RATING | ☆ ☆ ☆ ☆ ☆ |
| NOTES | | | |

| MOVIE TITLE | | DATE WATCHED | |
|---|---|---|---|
| GENRE | | RATING | ☆ ☆ ☆ ☆ ☆ |
| NOTES | | | |

| MOVIE TITLE | | DATE WATCHED | |
|---|---|---|---|
| GENRE | | RATING | ☆ ☆ ☆ ☆ ☆ |
| NOTES | | | |

| MOVIE TITLE | | DATE WATCHED | |
|---|---|---|---|
| GENRE | | RATING | ☆ ☆ ☆ ☆ ☆ |
| NOTES | | | |

| MOVIE TITLE | | DATE WATCHED | |
|---|---|---|---|
| GENRE | | RATING | ☆ ☆ ☆ ☆ ☆ |
| NOTES | | | |

# My Movie Tracker

| MOVIE TITLE | | DATE WATCHED | |
|---|---|---|---|
| GENRE | | RATING | ☆ ☆ ☆ ☆ ☆ |
| NOTES | | | |

| MOVIE TITLE | | DATE WATCHED | |
|---|---|---|---|
| GENRE | | RATING | ☆ ☆ ☆ ☆ ☆ |
| NOTES | | | |

| MOVIE TITLE | | DATE WATCHED | |
|---|---|---|---|
| GENRE | | RATING | ☆ ☆ ☆ ☆ ☆ |
| NOTES | | | |

| MOVIE TITLE | | DATE WATCHED | |
|---|---|---|---|
| GENRE | | RATING | ☆ ☆ ☆ ☆ ☆ |
| NOTES | | | |

| MOVIE TITLE | | DATE WATCHED | |
|---|---|---|---|
| GENRE | | RATING | ☆ ☆ ☆ ☆ ☆ |
| NOTES | | | |

| MOVIE TITLE | | DATE WATCHED | |
|---|---|---|---|
| GENRE | | RATING | ☆ ☆ ☆ ☆ ☆ |
| NOTES | | | |

| MOVIE TITLE | | DATE WATCHED | |
|---|---|---|---|
| GENRE | | RATING | ☆ ☆ ☆ ☆ ☆ |
| NOTES | | | |

| MOVIE TITLE | | DATE WATCHED | |
|---|---|---|---|
| GENRE | | RATING | ☆ ☆ ☆ ☆ ☆ |
| NOTES | | | |

# My Movie Tracker

| MOVIE TITLE | | DATE WATCHED | |
|---|---|---|---|
| GENRE | | RATING | ☆ ☆ ☆ ☆ ☆ |
| NOTES | | | |

| MOVIE TITLE | | DATE WATCHED | |
|---|---|---|---|
| GENRE | | RATING | ☆ ☆ ☆ ☆ ☆ |
| NOTES | | | |

| MOVIE TITLE | | DATE WATCHED | |
|---|---|---|---|
| GENRE | | RATING | ☆ ☆ ☆ ☆ ☆ |
| NOTES | | | |

| MOVIE TITLE | | DATE WATCHED | |
|---|---|---|---|
| GENRE | | RATING | ☆ ☆ ☆ ☆ ☆ |
| NOTES | | | |

| MOVIE TITLE | | DATE WATCHED | |
|---|---|---|---|
| GENRE | | RATING | ☆ ☆ ☆ ☆ ☆ |
| NOTES | | | |

| MOVIE TITLE | | DATE WATCHED | |
|---|---|---|---|
| GENRE | | RATING | ☆ ☆ ☆ ☆ ☆ |
| NOTES | | | |

| MOVIE TITLE | | DATE WATCHED | |
|---|---|---|---|
| GENRE | | RATING | ☆ ☆ ☆ ☆ ☆ |
| NOTES | | | |

| MOVIE TITLE | | DATE WATCHED | |
|---|---|---|---|
| GENRE | | RATING | ☆ ☆ ☆ ☆ ☆ |
| NOTES | | | |

# My Movie Tracker

| MOVIE TITLE | | DATE WATCHED | |
|---|---|---|---|
| GENRE | | RATING | ☆ ☆ ☆ ☆ ☆ |
| NOTES | | | |

| MOVIE TITLE | | DATE WATCHED | |
|---|---|---|---|
| GENRE | | RATING | ☆ ☆ ☆ ☆ ☆ |
| NOTES | | | |

| MOVIE TITLE | | DATE WATCHED | |
|---|---|---|---|
| GENRE | | RATING | ☆ ☆ ☆ ☆ ☆ |
| NOTES | | | |

| MOVIE TITLE | | DATE WATCHED | |
|---|---|---|---|
| GENRE | | RATING | ☆ ☆ ☆ ☆ ☆ |
| NOTES | | | |

| MOVIE TITLE | | DATE WATCHED | |
|---|---|---|---|
| GENRE | | RATING | ☆ ☆ ☆ ☆ ☆ |
| NOTES | | | |

| MOVIE TITLE | | DATE WATCHED | |
|---|---|---|---|
| GENRE | | RATING | ☆ ☆ ☆ ☆ ☆ |
| NOTES | | | |

| MOVIE TITLE | | DATE WATCHED | |
|---|---|---|---|
| GENRE | | RATING | ☆ ☆ ☆ ☆ ☆ |
| NOTES | | | |

| MOVIE TITLE | | DATE WATCHED | |
|---|---|---|---|
| GENRE | | RATING | ☆ ☆ ☆ ☆ ☆ |
| NOTES | | | |

# My Movie Tracker

| MOVIE TITLE | | DATE WATCHED | |
|---|---|---|---|
| GENRE | | RATING | ☆ ☆ ☆ ☆ ☆ |
| NOTES | | | |

| MOVIE TITLE | | DATE WATCHED | |
|---|---|---|---|
| GENRE | | RATING | ☆ ☆ ☆ ☆ ☆ |
| NOTES | | | |

| MOVIE TITLE | | DATE WATCHED | |
|---|---|---|---|
| GENRE | | RATING | ☆ ☆ ☆ ☆ ☆ |
| NOTES | | | |

| MOVIE TITLE | | DATE WATCHED | |
|---|---|---|---|
| GENRE | | RATING | ☆ ☆ ☆ ☆ ☆ |
| NOTES | | | |

| MOVIE TITLE | | DATE WATCHED | |
|---|---|---|---|
| GENRE | | RATING | ☆ ☆ ☆ ☆ ☆ |
| NOTES | | | |

| MOVIE TITLE | | DATE WATCHED | |
|---|---|---|---|
| GENRE | | RATING | ☆ ☆ ☆ ☆ ☆ |
| NOTES | | | |

| MOVIE TITLE | | DATE WATCHED | |
|---|---|---|---|
| GENRE | | RATING | ☆ ☆ ☆ ☆ ☆ |
| NOTES | | | |

| MOVIE TITLE | | DATE WATCHED | |
|---|---|---|---|
| GENRE | | RATING | ☆ ☆ ☆ ☆ ☆ |
| NOTES | | | |

# My Movie Tracker

| MOVIE TITLE | | DATE WATCHED | |
|---|---|---|---|
| GENRE | | RATING | ☆ ☆ ☆ ☆ ☆ |
| NOTES | | | |

| MOVIE TITLE | | DATE WATCHED | |
|---|---|---|---|
| GENRE | | RATING | ☆ ☆ ☆ ☆ ☆ |
| NOTES | | | |

| MOVIE TITLE | | DATE WATCHED | |
|---|---|---|---|
| GENRE | | RATING | ☆ ☆ ☆ ☆ ☆ |
| NOTES | | | |

| MOVIE TITLE | | DATE WATCHED | |
|---|---|---|---|
| GENRE | | RATING | ☆ ☆ ☆ ☆ ☆ |
| NOTES | | | |

| MOVIE TITLE | | DATE WATCHED | |
|---|---|---|---|
| GENRE | | RATING | ☆ ☆ ☆ ☆ ☆ |
| NOTES | | | |

| MOVIE TITLE | | DATE WATCHED | |
|---|---|---|---|
| GENRE | | RATING | ☆ ☆ ☆ ☆ ☆ |
| NOTES | | | |

| MOVIE TITLE | | DATE WATCHED | |
|---|---|---|---|
| GENRE | | RATING | ☆ ☆ ☆ ☆ ☆ |
| NOTES | | | |

| MOVIE TITLE | | DATE WATCHED | |
|---|---|---|---|
| GENRE | | RATING | ☆ ☆ ☆ ☆ ☆ |
| NOTES | | | |

# My Movie Tracker

| MOVIE TITLE | | DATE WATCHED | |
|---|---|---|---|
| GENRE | | RATING | ☆☆☆☆☆ |
| NOTES | | | |

| MOVIE TITLE | | DATE WATCHED | |
|---|---|---|---|
| GENRE | | RATING | ☆☆☆☆☆ |
| NOTES | | | |

| MOVIE TITLE | | DATE WATCHED | |
|---|---|---|---|
| GENRE | | RATING | ☆☆☆☆☆ |
| NOTES | | | |

| MOVIE TITLE | | DATE WATCHED | |
|---|---|---|---|
| GENRE | | RATING | ☆☆☆☆☆ |
| NOTES | | | |

| MOVIE TITLE | | DATE WATCHED | |
|---|---|---|---|
| GENRE | | RATING | ☆☆☆☆☆ |
| NOTES | | | |

| MOVIE TITLE | | DATE WATCHED | |
|---|---|---|---|
| GENRE | | RATING | ☆☆☆☆☆ |
| NOTES | | | |

| MOVIE TITLE | | DATE WATCHED | |
|---|---|---|---|
| GENRE | | RATING | ☆☆☆☆☆ |
| NOTES | | | |

| MOVIE TITLE | | DATE WATCHED | |
|---|---|---|---|
| GENRE | | RATING | ☆☆☆☆☆ |
| NOTES | | | |

# My Movie Tracker

| MOVIE TITLE | | DATE WATCHED | |
|---|---|---|---|
| GENRE | | RATING | ☆ ☆ ☆ ☆ ☆ |
| NOTES | | | |

| MOVIE TITLE | | DATE WATCHED | |
|---|---|---|---|
| GENRE | | RATING | ☆ ☆ ☆ ☆ ☆ |
| NOTES | | | |

| MOVIE TITLE | | DATE WATCHED | |
|---|---|---|---|
| GENRE | | RATING | ☆ ☆ ☆ ☆ ☆ |
| NOTES | | | |

| MOVIE TITLE | | DATE WATCHED | |
|---|---|---|---|
| GENRE | | RATING | ☆ ☆ ☆ ☆ ☆ |
| NOTES | | | |

| MOVIE TITLE | | DATE WATCHED | |
|---|---|---|---|
| GENRE | | RATING | ☆ ☆ ☆ ☆ ☆ |
| NOTES | | | |

| MOVIE TITLE | | DATE WATCHED | |
|---|---|---|---|
| GENRE | | RATING | ☆ ☆ ☆ ☆ ☆ |
| NOTES | | | |

| MOVIE TITLE | | DATE WATCHED | |
|---|---|---|---|
| GENRE | | RATING | ☆ ☆ ☆ ☆ ☆ |
| NOTES | | | |

| MOVIE TITLE | | DATE WATCHED | |
|---|---|---|---|
| GENRE | | RATING | ☆ ☆ ☆ ☆ ☆ |
| NOTES | | | |

# My Movie Tracker

| MOVIE TITLE | | DATE WATCHED | |
|---|---|---|---|
| GENRE | | RATING | ☆☆☆☆☆ |
| NOTES | | | |

| MOVIE TITLE | | DATE WATCHED | |
|---|---|---|---|
| GENRE | | RATING | ☆☆☆☆☆ |
| NOTES | | | |

| MOVIE TITLE | | DATE WATCHED | |
|---|---|---|---|
| GENRE | | RATING | ☆☆☆☆☆ |
| NOTES | | | |

| MOVIE TITLE | | DATE WATCHED | |
|---|---|---|---|
| GENRE | | RATING | ☆☆☆☆☆ |
| NOTES | | | |

| MOVIE TITLE | | DATE WATCHED | |
|---|---|---|---|
| GENRE | | RATING | ☆☆☆☆☆ |
| NOTES | | | |

| MOVIE TITLE | | DATE WATCHED | |
|---|---|---|---|
| GENRE | | RATING | ☆☆☆☆☆ |
| NOTES | | | |

| MOVIE TITLE | | DATE WATCHED | |
|---|---|---|---|
| GENRE | | RATING | ☆☆☆☆☆ |
| NOTES | | | |

| MOVIE TITLE | | DATE WATCHED | |
|---|---|---|---|
| GENRE | | RATING | ☆☆☆☆☆ |
| NOTES | | | |

# My Movie Tracker

| MOVIE TITLE | | DATE WATCHED | |
|---|---|---|---|
| GENRE | | RATING | ☆ ☆ ☆ ☆ ☆ |
| NOTES | | | |

| MOVIE TITLE | | DATE WATCHED | |
|---|---|---|---|
| GENRE | | RATING | ☆ ☆ ☆ ☆ ☆ |
| NOTES | | | |

| MOVIE TITLE | | DATE WATCHED | |
|---|---|---|---|
| GENRE | | RATING | ☆ ☆ ☆ ☆ ☆ |
| NOTES | | | |

| MOVIE TITLE | | DATE WATCHED | |
|---|---|---|---|
| GENRE | | RATING | ☆ ☆ ☆ ☆ ☆ |
| NOTES | | | |

| MOVIE TITLE | | DATE WATCHED | |
|---|---|---|---|
| GENRE | | RATING | ☆ ☆ ☆ ☆ ☆ |
| NOTES | | | |

| MOVIE TITLE | | DATE WATCHED | |
|---|---|---|---|
| GENRE | | RATING | ☆ ☆ ☆ ☆ ☆ |
| NOTES | | | |

| MOVIE TITLE | | DATE WATCHED | |
|---|---|---|---|
| GENRE | | RATING | ☆ ☆ ☆ ☆ ☆ |
| NOTES | | | |

| MOVIE TITLE | | DATE WATCHED | |
|---|---|---|---|
| GENRE | | RATING | ☆ ☆ ☆ ☆ ☆ |
| NOTES | | | |

# My Movie Tracker

| MOVIE TITLE | | DATE WATCHED | |
|---|---|---|---|
| GENRE | | RATING | ☆ ☆ ☆ ☆ ☆ |
| NOTES | | | |

| MOVIE TITLE | | DATE WATCHED | |
|---|---|---|---|
| GENRE | | RATING | ☆ ☆ ☆ ☆ ☆ |
| NOTES | | | |

| MOVIE TITLE | | DATE WATCHED | |
|---|---|---|---|
| GENRE | | RATING | ☆ ☆ ☆ ☆ ☆ |
| NOTES | | | |

| MOVIE TITLE | | DATE WATCHED | |
|---|---|---|---|
| GENRE | | RATING | ☆ ☆ ☆ ☆ ☆ |
| NOTES | | | |

| MOVIE TITLE | | DATE WATCHED | |
|---|---|---|---|
| GENRE | | RATING | ☆ ☆ ☆ ☆ ☆ |
| NOTES | | | |

| MOVIE TITLE | | DATE WATCHED | |
|---|---|---|---|
| GENRE | | RATING | ☆ ☆ ☆ ☆ ☆ |
| NOTES | | | |

| MOVIE TITLE | | DATE WATCHED | |
|---|---|---|---|
| GENRE | | RATING | ☆ ☆ ☆ ☆ ☆ |
| NOTES | | | |

| MOVIE TITLE | | DATE WATCHED | |
|---|---|---|---|
| GENRE | | RATING | ☆ ☆ ☆ ☆ ☆ |
| NOTES | | | |

# My Movie Tracker

| MOVIE TITLE | | DATE WATCHED | |
|---|---|---|---|
| GENRE | | RATING | ☆ ☆ ☆ ☆ ☆ |
| NOTES | | | |

| MOVIE TITLE | | DATE WATCHED | |
|---|---|---|---|
| GENRE | | RATING | ☆ ☆ ☆ ☆ ☆ |
| NOTES | | | |

| MOVIE TITLE | | DATE WATCHED | |
|---|---|---|---|
| GENRE | | RATING | ☆ ☆ ☆ ☆ ☆ |
| NOTES | | | |

| MOVIE TITLE | | DATE WATCHED | |
|---|---|---|---|
| GENRE | | RATING | ☆ ☆ ☆ ☆ ☆ |
| NOTES | | | |

| MOVIE TITLE | | DATE WATCHED | |
|---|---|---|---|
| GENRE | | RATING | ☆ ☆ ☆ ☆ ☆ |
| NOTES | | | |

| MOVIE TITLE | | DATE WATCHED | |
|---|---|---|---|
| GENRE | | RATING | ☆ ☆ ☆ ☆ ☆ |
| NOTES | | | |

| MOVIE TITLE | | DATE WATCHED | |
|---|---|---|---|
| GENRE | | RATING | ☆ ☆ ☆ ☆ ☆ |
| NOTES | | | |

| MOVIE TITLE | | DATE WATCHED | |
|---|---|---|---|
| GENRE | | RATING | ☆ ☆ ☆ ☆ ☆ |
| NOTES | | | |

# My Movie Tracker

| MOVIE TITLE | | DATE WATCHED | |
|---|---|---|---|
| GENRE | | RATING | ☆ ☆ ☆ ☆ ☆ |
| NOTES | | | |

| MOVIE TITLE | | DATE WATCHED | |
|---|---|---|---|
| GENRE | | RATING | ☆ ☆ ☆ ☆ ☆ |
| NOTES | | | |

| MOVIE TITLE | | DATE WATCHED | |
|---|---|---|---|
| GENRE | | RATING | ☆ ☆ ☆ ☆ ☆ |
| NOTES | | | |

| MOVIE TITLE | | DATE WATCHED | |
|---|---|---|---|
| GENRE | | RATING | ☆ ☆ ☆ ☆ ☆ |
| NOTES | | | |

| MOVIE TITLE | | DATE WATCHED | |
|---|---|---|---|
| GENRE | | RATING | ☆ ☆ ☆ ☆ ☆ |
| NOTES | | | |

| MOVIE TITLE | | DATE WATCHED | |
|---|---|---|---|
| GENRE | | RATING | ☆ ☆ ☆ ☆ ☆ |
| NOTES | | | |

| MOVIE TITLE | | DATE WATCHED | |
|---|---|---|---|
| GENRE | | RATING | ☆ ☆ ☆ ☆ ☆ |
| NOTES | | | |

| MOVIE TITLE | | DATE WATCHED | |
|---|---|---|---|
| GENRE | | RATING | ☆ ☆ ☆ ☆ ☆ |
| NOTES | | | |

# My Movie Tracker

| MOVIE TITLE | | DATE WATCHED | |
|---|---|---|---|
| GENRE | | RATING | ☆ ☆ ☆ ☆ ☆ |
| NOTES | | | |

| MOVIE TITLE | | DATE WATCHED | |
|---|---|---|---|
| GENRE | | RATING | ☆ ☆ ☆ ☆ ☆ |
| NOTES | | | |

| MOVIE TITLE | | DATE WATCHED | |
|---|---|---|---|
| GENRE | | RATING | ☆ ☆ ☆ ☆ ☆ |
| NOTES | | | |

| MOVIE TITLE | | DATE WATCHED | |
|---|---|---|---|
| GENRE | | RATING | ☆ ☆ ☆ ☆ ☆ |
| NOTES | | | |

| MOVIE TITLE | | DATE WATCHED | |
|---|---|---|---|
| GENRE | | RATING | ☆ ☆ ☆ ☆ ☆ |
| NOTES | | | |

| MOVIE TITLE | | DATE WATCHED | |
|---|---|---|---|
| GENRE | | RATING | ☆ ☆ ☆ ☆ ☆ |
| NOTES | | | |

| MOVIE TITLE | | DATE WATCHED | |
|---|---|---|---|
| GENRE | | RATING | ☆ ☆ ☆ ☆ ☆ |
| NOTES | | | |

| MOVIE TITLE | | DATE WATCHED | |
|---|---|---|---|
| GENRE | | RATING | ☆ ☆ ☆ ☆ ☆ |
| NOTES | | | |

# My Movie Tracker

| MOVIE TITLE | | DATE WATCHED | |
|---|---|---|---|
| GENRE | | RATING | ☆ ☆ ☆ ☆ ☆ |
| NOTES | | | |

| MOVIE TITLE | | DATE WATCHED | |
|---|---|---|---|
| GENRE | | RATING | ☆ ☆ ☆ ☆ ☆ |
| NOTES | | | |

| MOVIE TITLE | | DATE WATCHED | |
|---|---|---|---|
| GENRE | | RATING | ☆ ☆ ☆ ☆ ☆ |
| NOTES | | | |

| MOVIE TITLE | | DATE WATCHED | |
|---|---|---|---|
| GENRE | | RATING | ☆ ☆ ☆ ☆ ☆ |
| NOTES | | | |

| MOVIE TITLE | | DATE WATCHED | |
|---|---|---|---|
| GENRE | | RATING | ☆ ☆ ☆ ☆ ☆ |
| NOTES | | | |

| MOVIE TITLE | | DATE WATCHED | |
|---|---|---|---|
| GENRE | | RATING | ☆ ☆ ☆ ☆ ☆ |
| NOTES | | | |

| MOVIE TITLE | | DATE WATCHED | |
|---|---|---|---|
| GENRE | | RATING | ☆ ☆ ☆ ☆ ☆ |
| NOTES | | | |

| MOVIE TITLE | | DATE WATCHED | |
|---|---|---|---|
| GENRE | | RATING | ☆ ☆ ☆ ☆ ☆ |
| NOTES | | | |

www.ingramcontent.com/pod-product-compliance
Lightning Source LLC
Chambersburg PA
CBHW081232080526
44587CB00022B/3911